AMERICAN
MYTHS

AMERICAN

WHAT CANADIANS
THINK THEY KNOW
ABOUT THE UNITED STATES

MYTHS

EDITED BY
RUDYARD GRIFFITHS

KEY PORTER BOOKS

Library and Archives Canada Cataloguing in Publication

American myths : what Canadians think they know about the United States / Rudyard Griffiths, editor.

ISBN 978-1-55263-983-2

1. United States—Civilization—21st century. 2. National characteristics, American. 3. United States—Foreign public opinion, Canadian. 4. Public opinion—Canada. I. Griffiths, Rudyard

E169.12.A427 2008   973.93   C2007-905425-0

ONTARIO ARTS COUNCIL
CONSEIL DES ARTS DE L'ONTARIO

The publisher gratefully acknowledges the support of the Canada Council for the Arts and the Ontario Arts Council for its publishing program. We acknowledge the support of the Government of Ontario through the Ontario Media Development Corporation's Ontario Book Initiative.

We acknowledge the financial support of the Government of Canada through the Book Publishing Industry Development Program (BPIDP) for our publishing activities.

Key Porter Books Limited
Six Adelaide Street East, Tenth Floor
Toronto, Ontario
Canada M5C 1H6

www.keyporter.com

Text design: Marijke Friesen
Electronic formatting: Alison Carr

Printed and bound in Canada

08 09 10 11 12 5 4 3 2 1

CONTENTS

ACKNOWLEDGEMENTS

THE PUBLICATION OF THIS BOOK would not have been possible without the contributions of a remarkable group of public-spirited individuals and groups. In addition to all of the authors who contributed to *American Myths*, the Dominion Institute would like to thank the *National Post* and its editor-in-chief Douglas Kelly for publishing edited versions of five of the essays that appear in *American Myths*. The public discussion elicited by the original *National Post* series was instrumental in helping the Dominion Institute garner the financial support to significantly expand the essays that first appeared in the newspaper and involve an entirely new and expanded group of contributors.

The Donner Canadian Foundation, the patron saint of public policy debate and research in Canada, provided the majority of the funding for this publication. The Dominion Institute especially wishes to thank the Donner Foundation's chair, Allan Gotlieb, and board members Joseph Donner Jr. and Belinda Donner for their outstanding support. We would also like to thank our editor at Key Porter Books, Linda Pruessen, and acknowledge the financial contribution of Key Porter to this publication. We salute their ongoing investment in publishing, in Canada, and in books on public policy themes.

Finally, the Dominion Institute would like to give special

thanks to Pat Kennedy, who acted as the Institute's "in-house" editor on this book and worked tirelessly to cajole authors, polish manuscripts, and keep all of us on schedule and on budget.

The Dominion Institute is a national charity founded in 1997 by a group of young people to promote greater knowledge of Canadian history and the informed discussion of public-policy issues in Canada. For more information on the Dominion Institute please visit our website: www.dominion.ca.

INTRODUCTION

BY RUDYARD GRIFFITHS

I CAN HEAR THE SCRATCHING OF HEADS in university common rooms, in government offices along the banks of the Rideau River, and within nationalist bastions such as the Council of Canadians. These and other people are asking themselves: what has the Dominion Institute gone and done?

Specifically, why has an organization that has spent the last decade championing Canadian history and the informed debate of public policy issues in Canada published a book all about America? Even more bizarre, why is the pro–Canada Dominion Institute encouraging Canadian and American writers to explore, among other things, what the American health-care system can teach us about caring for an aging population, why large U.S. cities are overtaking their Canadian counterparts not just in terms of economic growth but quality of life too, and, horror of horrors, how American environmental policies could be adapted to Canada to fight climate change. Either the world has suddenly turned on its head or the brain trust at the Dominion Institute has come down with an acute case of beaver fever.

Rest assured, the publication of this book is motivated by the Dominion Institute's long-standing concern for all things Canadian. *American Myths* was inspired by our belief that too many of our political discussions and too much of our analysis of how best to tackle the major forces transforming our country are hamstrung by a knee-jerk and unproductive anti-Americanism that permeates our national conversation.

Every Canadian is familiar with this particular cultural tic. If an aspiring political leader is foolish enough to publicly advocate that market mechanisms, such as U.S.-style user fees, should be used to increase the efficiency of public health care, they become ineligible to hold elected office. The same rule of thumb applies to urban policy. According to a host of indicators, we know that big American cities are outperforming their Canadian counterparts. Yet woe betide the think tank or journalist who points out these gaping discrepancies. In our imaginations Toronto, Montreal, and Vancouver are not twenty years out of date in terms of their urban planning and all Americans still live in vast soulless suburbs around rotting city cores. This same dynamic of distorting our perceptions of ourselves by misconstruing all things American is front and centre in how we think about national defence and foreign affairs. Here the stereotype is that Canada is the nation of "peacekeepers" and Americans are the "war makers." These myths continue to dominate how we perceive our role in the world despite the fact that less than two hundred Canadians served on U.N. peacekeeping missions last year and that the U.S. remains the world's largest humanitarian and foreign-aid donor, bar none.

The examples of how Canadians' misperceptions about America forestall or narrow our political and policy debates about everything from multiculturalism to aboriginal policy are legion. They are also harmful—a tragic diversion from the hard but necessary work of defining who we are as a country on our own terms. I believe that, if we are to have any hope of resolving the complex issues swirling around our strained health-care system, endemic aboriginal poverty, or stressed urban centres, we must overcome our innate sense of moral superiority vis-à-vis the United States and borrow the best ideas from wherever we can find them—including America.

American Myths is nothing less, and nothing more, than the Dominion Institute's contribution to the project of freeing Canadians from the intellectual straitjacket of anti-Americanism. Given our deeply ingrained habit of caricaturizing American society while being far too tolerant about our own faults and foibles, the essays contained in this book are purposely provocative. Each author was given the assignment of picking what they consider to be a key aspect of American society or U.S. policy most often misunderstood or misconstrued by Canadians. Contributors were also encouraged not to simply set the record straight but also suggest how Canadians could learn from the American experience and adapt U.S. policies to the Canadian context.

And so, for instance, we have Dr. David Gratzer arguing that, far from being compassionless, American health care is producing better results than our overstretched Canadian system, and is covering a good portion of the underprivileged. Dr. Gratzer shows how various aspects of the U.S. system could be adapted to Canada to increase the quality of patient care and control the spiralling costs associated with treating our aging population without curtailing Canadians' overall health-care coverage.

We have Neil Reynolds commenting unfavourably on the hypocrisy of Canadian politicians that lecture the United States on its lack of a global conscience over the Kyoto Protocol, ignoring the fact that the Americans have done better at cutting harmful emissions than has Canada. He argues that, if we can resist the temptation to make snap judgments about the supposed failure of American environmental policy, Canada could learn a number of valuable lessons about how to reduce our greenhouse-gas emissions.

There are also some essayists that tackle what they consider a few home truths in the Canadian–American relationship.

We have J.L. Granatstein proclaiming that, militarily, Canada has "largely had a free ride, while the United States took most of the risks, paid the lion's share of the bills, and, for its pains, bore the brunt of the world's abuse." Perhaps, he argues, it would behoove us to cooperate with our neighbour when it serves our national interests.

Allan Gotlieb, Canada's former ambassador in Washington would no doubt agree, as he lays out the many occasions (seemingly forgotten) when the Americans went out of their way to consider Canada's interests in the decades before Pierre Trudeau placed Canadian–American relations low on his list of government priorities.

Taken together, the essays that make up *American Myths* provide a fresh perspective on the range of practical solutions and different kinds of thinking in America that Canadian government and civil society could bring to bear on the major challenges facing Canada. Just as important, they also convey a powerful sense of the costs to good policy-making in Canada caused by our tendency to adopt ideological positions on the ground that they run counter to U.S. models or the American experience.

I, for one, am optimistic that Canada is entering a more robust and confident phase of nationhood. Having not just survived but thrived as a people under free trade and head-to-head competition with the United States. I believe we are approaching a juncture in our history where public debate in Canada is increasingly unfolding on its own terms, free of an anti-American tinge. This change is most evident in our foreign policy, where we have found the self-confidence to discuss the pros and cons of our military mission in Afghanistan mostly in terms of Canada's national interests and values as opposed to seeing our involvement in the war-torn country as either part of an American conspiracy to ensnare Canada in George Bush's so-called "War on Terror" or a ploy to improve Canada–U.S. business relations. Such a shift, not just in the realms of foreign affairs and international relations but also domestic issues, can only be a good thing in that effective public policy is effective public policy, regardless of who thought it up. We all know that at the end of day, open and honest public discussion that brings forward the widest range of options, in the style and substance of *American Myths*, is in all of our interests.

Rudyard Griffiths
Erin, Ontario, 2008

AMERICAN
MYTHS

SOMETIMES MAKING PEACE MEANS MAKING WAR

BY J.L. GRANATSTEIN

"CANADIANS KEEP THE PEACE; Americans fight wars." That clichéd statement, that Canadian myth, is now accepted as gospel truth from St. John's to Quebec City and from Toronto to Vancouver. Canadians proudly cite Lester B. Pearson's Nobel Peace Prize, won for his role in creating the first large peacekeeping force and for stabilizing the Suez Crisis of 1956. They look at the Nobel Peace Prize that went to United Nations peacekeepers in 1988 and say, loudly, that it was really for Canada's soldiers. They point to the grand peacekeeping monument in Ottawa and to the back of their $10 bill showing Canadian peacekeepers. We are the good guys in white hats—or, at least, blue berets. Canadians, we appear to think, are natural-born peacekeepers, the world's ideal middlemen.

And the Yanks? America, by contrast, is the superpower that fought in Vietnam and used Agent Orange to defoliate the jungle—and to cause illnesses years later. Americans waged war against the Nicaraguan, Grenadian, Panamanian, and Cuban peoples, invaded Iraq twice in the last decade and a half, and continue to station troops, ships, and aircraft all over the world to serve U.S. interests and ensure control over the oil supplies they need to drive their gas-guzzling automobiles. If we're the good guys, surely the Americans are the world's bullies, the target of every terrorist group that aims to draw attention to its grievances. Too many Canadians accept this view of their neighbours. It took some Canadians little more than a day to say that the deaths in New York and Washington from the terror attacks of 9/11 served the Americans right.

Yes, the Americans are a troublesome people. They are suffused with a grandiose sense of their exceptionalism and mission, their manifest destiny to make the world's peoples more like them, with a McDonald's in every European town and Coke in every grocery store in Indonesia. They preach freedom and democracy in loud terms, while packing assault rifles in their suvs and consuming most of the world's resources. They brag and boast about everything, wallow in religiosity, and wave the flag at every opportunity. Bullies, braggarts, warmongers!

But let's look at the last hundred years of history. Would the Allies have won the Great War if Woodrow Wilson's America, promising a war to end all wars and pressing idealistically for the creation of a League of Nations, had not entered the conflict in April 1917 and put more than a million men into the fray? Would the Second World War have been a triumph for Adolf Hitler, Benito Mussolini, and Hideki Tojo if America had not sent its soldiers and sailors and the products of its factories and fields to war? Would the Soviet Union and Communist China not have seized every state in Europe and Asia if the United States had not galvanized the creation of the North Atlantic Treaty and provided most of the power and much of the money for its armies? If the United States had not put its blood and treasure on the line in Korea? If the United States had not been the rallying point for freedom for a century and more?

Yes, we Canadians have done our part in the great conflicts too. There are more than one hundred thousand dead soldiers, sailors, and airmen to testify to Canada's commitment to freedom and democracy, and billions of dollars from the nation's treasury went to hold off the world's enemies. But Canada is a small, relatively weak country, and the United States is a superpower. However much Canada contributed its men and produced the machines of war, none of it would have mattered much without the support of allies. And the most powerful ally, the indispensable ally in preserving democracy and freedom, without question, was and remains the United States.

Yet Canadians jeer and sneer at their neighbours. They were late into the First World War and then claimed they had won it. They were late again in the Second World War and once again believed that they had saved Britain's bacon. In the Korean War that began in 1950, Canadian foreign minister Mike Pearson pressed so hard at the United Nations for a truce that the Americans came to resent his preaching and prodding bitterly. Those moralistic Canadians were at it again, that "stern daughter of the voice of God," as U.S. secretary of state Dean Acheson later wrote, carping endlessly about Canada's moral superiority while the United States paid most of the price in blood and treasure.

But unhappy as they may have been over the Canadian position on a Korean armistice, the Americans did listen to Canada at the United Nations and in Washington. Ottawa had earned the right to be heard by sending a brigade group of five thousand soldiers to fight in Korea, by dispatching destroyers to serve off the coast of that Asian peninsula, and by using the Royal Canadian Air Force's transports to ferry men and supplies to the Far East. Canada paid its dues in the war and, because it did, Washington, however grumpily and reluctantly, heard the nation's voice. It didn't always listen, but the Americans recognized our right to offer our views.

A few years later, the United States even accepted Canada's demands that the air defence of North America, the defence of their own soil, be shared. The North American Air Defence Command, created in 1957–58, was a joint operation with Canadian officers sitting side by side with their U.S. counterparts at NORAD headquarters in Colorado Springs. But when the Cuban missile crisis exploded in the fall of 1962, and North America was threatened by a Soviet nuclear attack, the Canadian public belatedly realized that their country's surface-to-air missiles were unarmed, their aircraft ill-equipped for war, and their government reluctant even to put its military on full alert. The Americans did the heavy lifting, just as they had always done, and they were not happy that John Diefenbaker's Ottawa had let them down in the greatest crisis of the Cold War.

Canada had become tired of the Cold War. Our governments didn't want to pay the bills for real defence. Our politicians sought after Nobel Prizes by tilting towards neutrality in the Cold War and by proclaiming Canada's moral superpower status. And over time, the country's military contributions to the North Atlantic Treaty Organization's forces in Europe were trimmed, cut, slashed by half, and finally, in 1993, eliminated entirely. Let someone else pay the bills, our prime ministers said, taking their peace dividend well before the end of the Cold War. If the United States wanted to be a superpower, always flexing its muscles, let U.S. taxpayers carry the can. And they did.

Ah, but, Canadians say, when their slackness in defence is pointed out, we are the world's pre-eminent peacekeepers. The Americans fought the wars, sure, but we kept the peace. That was useful, wasn't it? Everyone loved us, didn't they?

Well, sort of. For years from 1950 onwards, Canadians claimed that they were the only nation to be represented in every United Nations peacekeeping mission. Kashmir, the Israeli–Arab borders, Cyprus, Yemen, West New Guinea— the list went on and on. The record was good, no doubt about it, but Canadians forget too much. Most of the crises were frozen but never resolved, and most of the missions went on forever—until the parties involved had re-armed and recovered sufficiently to resume hostilities. Canada went to Cyprus in 1964 and finally pulled out, completely frustrated, three decades later; the political struggle there between Greek and Turkish Cypriots continues still. The Arab–Israeli conflict is never-ending, and the tussle between nuclear-armed India and Pakistan over Kashmir can flare up at any moment, and likely will. Peacekeeping was "a good thing," of course, but without peacemaking, without efforts to force all parties towards a resolution, it simply didn't work. Canada never had the power to impose peace, and the United Nations Security Council, which did, never had the will.

Moreover, peacekeeping was never really impartial, with Canadian soldiers playing the neutral middleman role most thought we did. We went to Cyprus, for example, because U.S. president Lyndon Johnson begged us to do so, and because Greece and Turkey were NATO allies; if they had gone to war over the Mediterranean island, the whole of the Alliance's southern flank would have been irreparably damaged. Nor was peacekeeping something we ever did on our own. When the Canadian Forces deployed to Suez in 1956, for example, American stockpiles of equipment were needed; similarly, when the Canadian Forces sent army signallers to the Iran–Iraq border after the end of Saddam Hussein's war against the Iranian mullahs in 1988, American aircraft had to be employed to carry their heavy equipment. Canadian radios, it turned out, wouldn't work in the mountainous regions, so the U.S. military provided radio sets for the Canadian contingent. This ought to have been a national embarrassment, but the Canadian public paid no attention, instead basking delightedly in the kudos offered for yet another peacekeeping mission.

And when the Cold War ended at the beginning of the 1990s, and the heavy hands of Moscow and Washington were removed from long-suppressed tribal and racial nationalisms, traditional peacekeeping quickly morphed into more vigorous, more dangerous peacemaking and peace enforcement. Canada suddenly discovered that its shrunken military was under strength, and too ill-equipped to do the job for long. In Somalia, the Canadian Airborne Regiment saw two of its soldiers murder a young boy, an event that provoked a massive political and military cover-up, and, after a soul-searing commission of inquiry, the unit was ultimately disbanded. Our troops serving in the former Yugoslavia performed well, but unfortunately—to our allies—they seemed to be hampered by Ottawa's restrictive rules of engagement and their shoddy equipment. The unit deployed there was labelled a "Canbat" by Ottawa, short for "Canadian battalion." British soldiers serving near the Canadian contingent were quick to call the unit the "Can't Bat." That was no compliment.

Then, when a single infantry battalion was dispatched to Afghanistan in 2002 to serve under U.S. command in the war against Taliban terrorism, the soldiers of the Third battalion of the Princess Patricia's Canadian Light Infantry had the wrong uniforms and boots for desert conditions and had to rely on the U.S. forces for helicopters and close air support. And when, tragically, four Canadian soldiers died in a "friendly fire" bombing by U.S. air force fighters, the cries that the Yanks were trigger-happy rose up very quickly and a successful deployment was all but destroyed by rampant anti-Americanism at home. The navy, the best-equipped of our services, carried out its role in the War on Terror with great success—but eventually had to withdraw from operations to give its over-stretched sailors a "pause." Canada a peacekeeper?

The army went back to Afghanistan in 2003, putting an infantry battalion onto the relatively safe streets of Kabul, a role close to traditional peacekeeping and one accepted so that Ottawa could say it was doing its bit—and to justify its decision to stay out of the Iraq War. Only in 2005–06 did Canada return to Afghanistan in force, with a 2,500-person unit, to direct a provincial reconstruction team in dangerous Kandahar province and to battle a resurgent Taliban. By early 2008, seventy-eight Canadian soldiers had been killed, and the government, driven by a divided public, was hard-pressed to keep the mission going.

The harsh truth is that Canada has largely had a free ride, while the United States took most of the risks, paid the lion's share of the bills, and, for its pains, bore the brunt of the world's abuse. The Canadian Forces, its strength of 63,000 men and women grossly inadequate to its tasks, its helicopters, air transports, replenishment ships, destroyers, army trucks, and artillery still obsolete, cannot even credibly defend this nation's air space, sea approaches, and land mass. The only question is how much longer the United States will wait before it declares that its own national security makes it necessary for Washington to put stringent controls on the Canada–U.S. border or, more forebodingly, to openly assume responsibility for Canadian defence. Can Canada still call itself a sovereign state if that occurs?

Our leaders seem blithely unaware of the realities. Prime Minister Paul Martin in 2005 decided that his government would not participate in ballistic missile defence with the United States. The Americans had not asked for any use of Canadian territory and they had not sought any cash contribution to the hugely expensive development of BMD. They simply wanted Ottawa's political support and, as we were their partners in the North American Aerospace Defense Command, they thought we might like a seat at the table if and when decisions needed to be taken as a North Korean or Iranian nuclear missile came over the horizon. There is no doubt that BMD is politically contentious in Europe and North America, no doubt that the technology has yet to be perfected, but also no doubt that there are threats to North America from "rogue" states. But those factors did not appear to shape the prime ministerial decision. What did was a coming federal election, the huge unpopularity among Canadian voters of the Bush administration, and the Liberal government's willingness to play to domestic anti-American sentiment.

By opting out of ballistic missile defence, Prime Minister Martin in effect turned over to the United States complete responsibility for the space defence of North America. The prime minister denied that this was so, but he dissembled and claimed that, of course, Canada would be involved in the defence of the continent against missile attack. How? If we had no seat at the BMD table, just how would Canada have a role? President Bush was said to have told the Canadian leader at a summit meeting, "I'm not taking this position, but some future president is going to say, 'Why are we paying to defend Canada?'" Perhaps not quite the buffoon Canadians usually paint him to be, Bush then added about BMD: "I don't understand this. Are you saying that if you got up and said this was necessary for the defence of Canada, it wouldn't be accepted?" Martin didn't respond. He couldn't. There is an unreality about the willingness of a Canadian prime minister to put transitory political advantage (which didn't work, as Martin lost the 2005–06 election and disappeared from the political scene) ahead of the essentials of national survival.

What makes Canada's weak sense of military necessity all the more remarkable is the nation's dependence on the United

States for its defence, yes, but also for its prosperity. Consider four economic statistics:

- 80 per cent of Canadian exports go to or through the United States;
- Canada–U.S. two-way trade amounts to more than $700 billion each year;
- Canada–U.S. trade makes up more than half of Canada's gross domestic product;
- and as many as 35 per cent of Canadian jobs depend on this trade.

Such statistics ought to concentrate our leaders' minds and oblige them—and the Canadian people—to recognize our dependence on the United States. We are North Americans, we share the continent with the United States, and we have responsibilities to protect and advance our shared interests. The consequences of failing to do so should be clear enough: the United States will be forced in its own interests to assume greater responsibilities in and over our territory, and we can be reduced to penury if the neighbouring superpower finally gets fed up with us. Neither is a desirable result for the great Canadian experiment of trying to build a different way of life in North America.

Canadians need to be more clear-headed about the world. They have national interests, not just values. They must defend them or see them overridden by others. The Americans have their own national interests, and today they believe rightly that terrorists everywhere are plotting ways to kill Americans. The

United States has demonstrated it will do what it deems necessary to protect its interests. Sometimes, the Americans make terrible mistakes, and Canadians will always let them know when they're wrong. The Bush–Cheney administration in particular has been a disaster at home and abroad, and Canadian scorn is always quick to be offered. But is abuse and shouting the way to be heard in Washington? Does anyone in Canada remember that Bush will be leaving office in January 2009, and that some Americans will remember the abuse more than the president at whom it was directed?

Perhaps, just perhaps, cooperating with the United States politically and militarily *when it serves Canada's interests* might be a better way to proceed. It worked for Mike Pearson during the Korean War. It might still work in a very different but no less dangerous world. The only test that matters is that of national interest. Is taking Course A rather than Course B best suited to advance our interests? Anti-Bush attitudes, anti-Americanism, might be part of the decision-making equation, but they alone cannot decide issues. Only national interests can do that.

Canada is part of Western civilization, and we share the values and beliefs of that civilization. So do Americans. We must get beyond the reflexive desire to criticize the superpower next door and understand that, if the United States is crippled, we too will suffer. We can pretend we keep the peace if it pleases us to do so, but we simply must recognize that, without America's strength and will, our civilization will disappear and the barbarians, already at our gates, will prevail. More realism, fewer myths, please.

THE JUST SOCIETY

BY DAVID FRUM

As HE OPENED HIS 2004 ELECTION CAMPAIGN, a scandal-battered Paul Martin reached for a time-tested election winner:

"I know the arithmetic of the tax-cut equation," he said. "You can have a country like Canada. You can have a country like the United States. That's a choice you can make. But you cannot have a health-care system like Canada's, and you cannot have social programs like Canada's, with taxation levels like those in the United States."

Now as a matter of literal truth, Martin's words were not quite accurate. Canadian federal and provincial governments that year spent just south of us$2,500 per person on health care. Multiplied by the 296 million people then living in the United States, that would translate to us$740 billion—or us$60 billion less than American federal and state governments spent in 2004 on their existing health programs.

Put it this way: Canada could have had American tax rates and the Canadian health-care system—if Canada had an economy as rich as that of the United States.

But if Martin's words were literally false, there is no doubt that they expressed a psychological truth. Many Canadians want to believe that America has a radically less just society than Canada—and Canadians most especially want to believe that when they notice that the American economy is out-performing Canada's, as it did throughout the years when Paul Martin was managing Canada's finances.

And so they tell themselves that America's lower taxes and higher GDP per capita, lower unemployment and faster growth are all achieved at the expense of more important values: equality, fairness, and health care for all.

And indeed, in some important ways, Canada does deliver better results to Canadians than U.S. society delivers to Americans. Crime is generally lower in Canada, as is infant mortality, as is child poverty. (In other respects, it should be said, Canada does worse: unemployment is higher in Canada, average incomes are lower both before and after taxes, and Canadians who suffer heart attacks and other illnesses requiring prompt medical attention are less likely to survive than their American neighbours.)

But is this "justice"?

Critics of American society have a habit of equating justice with equality—the more equal the society, the more just it is. By this criterion, Canada is more just than the United States, and France is more just than Canada, and Denmark is more just than France, and so on. By this same criterion, the Soviet Union was more just than post-Soviet Russia, Mao's Cultural Revolution was more just than Hong Kong, and North Korea more just than South Korea—and down the backward slide we go, from error to absurdity to horror.

Even if this way of thinking made sense, it would tell us little about the differences between the United States and Canada. Compared to any other advanced industrial societies, the most striking thing about the two great North American democracies is how very similar they are. They share relatively low levels of government involvement in the economy, relatively high levels of economic inequality, relatively high levels of gun ownership, relatively high levels of religiosity. The case that the United States is an "unjust" society cuts almost equally sharply against Canada as well.

It would be more sensible to think of equality as an independent social quality, one with both costs and benefits. Very extreme inequality—like that which is seen in Latin America or the Middle East—is certainly a social evil. It incites a dangerous radicalism among the poor and corrodes support for democracy among the rich. Extreme inequality corrodes social trust among citizens, exacerbates corruption, and impoverishes essential public services like education.

On the other hand, societies that enforce artificially high levels of equality also pay a price. Innovation and entrepreneurship decline, capital investment flees. The effects are mildest in small, ethnically homogeneous societies like Denmark, much more pronounced in larger and more diverse societies like France or Germany. It is never possible to have too much justice. But it is certainly possible to have too much equality.

There's another and better way to think of justice: a just society is not one that seeks to achieve fair results, but one that lives by fair rules, fairly enforced. The philosophers describe this kind of justice as commutative rather than distributive justice. Lawyers describe it as "the rule of law." Maybe it's most vividly summoned up by a British music-hall song from the 1930s, quoted in one of George Orwell's essays:

"Oh you can't do that here,
No you can't do that here.
Maybe you can do that over there,
But you can't do that here."

What is it that they can do over there—but can't do over here? Lawyers and philosophers have battled over precise definitions for centuries, but here are some of the main elements of a society under the rule of law:

1. The rules are equal: What is lawful for one person should be lawful for all; what is forbidden to one should be forbidden to all.
2. The rules are predictable: Individual rights and duties should be knowable in advance, and should not be changed after the fact without the individual's consent.
3. The rules are stable: When the rules change, they change only with enough notice, so that individuals can alter their behaviour in time.
4. The rules are supreme: Nobody can be punished unless they have violated one of those equal, predictable, and stable rules.

You can find some version of those rules in every bill of rights of every modern democracy, including Canada's. But it was the Americans who were the first to incorporate them into their fundamental law, 216 years ago. And even now, all these years later, the Americans still live by the principles of the rule of law more consistently than any other nation—and far more consistently, it is sobering to reflect, than Canadians ... despite Canada's free health care.

Take Principle 1, equality before the law. That principle has been bent in the United States by affirmative action and racial preferences, but it has not been utterly discarded. In her majority opinion in the 2004 case of *Grutter v. Bollinger*, which upheld racial preferences at the University of Michigan Law School, Sandra Day O'Connor opined that preferences should be seen as a temporary deviation from the enduring principles of equal justice. She warned that the court expected such preferences to disappear over the next twenty-five years, explaining: "Enshrining a permanent justification for racial preferences would offend this fundamental equal protection principle."

But Canada has enshrined permanent racial preferences into Canadian law.

In the words of Section 15 of the Canadian Charter of Rights and Freedoms:

1. Everyone has the right to equality before the law and to equal protection of the law without discrimination because of race, national or ethnic origin, colour, religion, age, or sex.
2. This section does not preclude any law, program, or activity that has as its object the amelioration of conditions of disadvantaged persons or groups.

Notice something especially shocking about the Subsection 2 exception to the general rule laid down in Subsection 1: the exceptions to the normal rule of law are not required to show any likelihood of actual success. The guarantee of equal treatment can be discarded by any law or agency that professes to be aimed at helping the disadvantaged. Good intentions are enough.

Nor is the concept of "amelioration" a very clear one. Suppose, for example, scientists were to develop a new gene therapy that could raise the IQs of gestating fetuses from subnormal to normal levels. Could the government of Canada require all expectant mothers with subnormal IQs to accept this therapy? Would that not count as "amelioration"?

These questions are not hypothetical. Canadian courts have already jettisoned the rule of equal treatment in a wide variety of cases, involving both Charter and non-Charter litigation.

- Canadian citizens of native origin, for example, may hunt and fish when and where other citizens cannot. (*R. v. Marshall,* 1999.)

- British Columbians of native origin may claim lands on the basis of oral evidence that would be thrown out of court if offered by a non-native. (*Delgamuukw v. British Columbia,* 1997.)

- Generally speaking, governments may legally discriminate in favour of certain groups in hiring, firing, and the distribution of public money. (*Lovelace v. Ontario,* 2000.)

The Canadian and American legal systems are likewise diverging in their respect for the stability and predictability of the law.

The U.S. Constitution prohibits ex-post-facto laws and forbids states to pass laws impairing the obligations of contracts. The U.S. Supreme Court has enforced this rule in even the most challenging and unappealing cases. Consider for example the 2000 case of *Carmell v. Texas*. Scott Carmell was accused of molesting his underage stepdaughter in the early 1990s. At that time, Texas law said that individuals accused of certain sexual crimes could not be convicted purely on the testimony of the alleged victim. There had to be some kind of corroborative evidence, either physical or else comments made at the time to some third party. Texas altered its law in 1993. In 1997, Carmell was prosecuted on molestation charges. The jury believed his stepdaughter's testimony and convicted him. The Supreme Court overturned his conviction, citing the ex-post-facto clause. The court ruled that not only does the Constitution forbid changing the law after the fact, but it forbids changing the rules of evidence that prove the law after the fact. That's a hard line.

Canadian courts have shown themselves more than willing to change the law after the fact, punishing and rewarding individuals in ways entirely unforeseen at the time.

In Canada, unmarried individuals have had the rights of marriage conferred on them and the obligations of marriage imposed upon them after the fact (*Miron v. Trudel*, 1995; *M. v. H.*, 1999). Private corporations have been punished for firing people they had every right to fire under the laws in place at the time (*Vriend v. Alberta*, 1998). And "final" marital separation agreements can be reopened by courts at any subsequent time, if those agreements are seen to disadvantage one spouse (*Miglin v. Miglin*, 2001)—although, as a practical matter, courts will only do so if the spouse is the wife.

The increasing divergence between American and Canadian norms of justice is not occurring by accident. The rule of law is a fundamentally individualist concept, and the ideal of justice protected by the rule of law is libertarian, not egalitarian. Canadian courts, by contrast, increasingly think in collectivist terms. If, in order to attain some vision of equality, men must be treated differently from women, or blacks from whites, or aboriginal Canadians from everybody else—well, so be it. Canada's newest Supreme Court justice, Rosalie Abella, warns that courts err when they have "allowed the individualism of civil liberties to trump the group realities of human rights."

Every legal system has its flaws and failures. The American civil-justice system wreaks plenty of havoc: Just a very few weeks ago, for example, the drug-maker Merck was hit with a $253 million judgment against its painkiller Vioxx, in a case marked by blithe disregard of scientific and medical evidence by a Texas jury. ("Jurors who voted against Merck said much of the science sailed right over their heads," reported the *Wall Street Journal*. "'Whenever Merck was up there, it was like wah, wah, wah,' said juror John Ostrom, imitating the sounds Charlie Brown's teacher makes in the television cartoon. 'We didn't know what the heck they were talking about.'")

Future presidential candidate John Edwards made his first fortune by convincing a jury that a botched delivery caused a baby's cerebral palsy—a scientific impossibility. Other lawyers have made multimillion-dollar fortunes out of asbestos, securities, and tobacco litigation that paid much more in attorney fees than they ever delivered in compensation to injured people.

Oftentimes, an American corporation can look forward to more even-handed and less emotional treatment from a Canadian judge than from an American jury. The defects of other legal systems are, however, weak condolence for the failures of one's own. "Justice, justice shalt thou pursue," decrees the lawgiver of Deuteronomy, and it is an obligation binding on each and every nation.

The United States has sought to pursue justice by adhering to the ancient ideals of the rule of law. Canada, like the social democracies of Europe, has attempted a different path. Justice has anciently been depicted blindfolded, weighing litigants in her scales without partiality. The Canadian ideal, however, increasingly demands that justice open her eyes—and put a thumb on the scales to assist her chosen favourites.

Some left-wing American lawyers have created a concept of "preferred rights" to justify attaching greater weight to the free-speech rights of the First Amendment than the gun rights guaranteed by the Second. Canadian courts seem to have arrived at a concept of preferred litigants, that grants outcomes to native, female, homosexual, or ethnic minority litigants that would never be extended to majority litigants.

Almost four decades ago, the most anti-American of all Canadian prime ministers urged Canadians to make themselves a "just society." It was never very clear what Pierre Trudeau meant by those words.

Trudeau and his supporters tried to use the language of

justice as a universal defence of everything they wanted to do. Did they prefer nationwide bilingualism rather than French predominance in Quebec and English predominance elsewhere? That was not linguistic policy: It was "justice." Did they want to increase social spending faster than total national income? That, too, was "justice." Did they prefer American-style jurisprudence to the tradition of judicial restraint inherited from Westminster? That was "justice" again.

In his last years, Trudeau often seemed embittered and exasperated. He looked and sounded like a man who considered his life's work a failure. One might think that he had little reason for those feelings: for better or for worse, he stamped Canada with his likeness in a way that no prime minister since John A. Macdonald had managed to do. But then again, maybe he had every reason for disappointment. His hopes and ideals were never realized, for the powerful reason that they were unrealizable. The attempt to rename every social policy, every political wish, as a requirement of "justice" meant that every compromise, every concession to political opponents or adverse reality, became an "injustice." Politics has famously been called the art of the possible. Pierre Trudeau's invocation of justice in every imaginable political context condemned his politics to be an exercise in the impossible.

In the political theory of limited government, "justice" is a meaningful concept, if a limited one. In the political theory of social democracy, "justice" extends to everything—it can never be achieved, society must always fall short, leaving society moving (in the title of a late-life collection of Trudeau's essays) always "towards" justice, without ever attaining it.

And ironically, the further opponents of the limited government tradition have tried to push nations "towards" the hazy
justice of their imaginations, the further they have drifted
from justice in the most fundamental and most important
meaning of the word in the civilization to which Canada
belongs.

AMERICA: HARDLY A MELTING POT …

BY PATRICK LUCIANI

ONCE UPON A TIME, I was an immigrant. But I've never referred to myself as one. Having come here as an infant, I've long identified more with my adopted country than the one I left—which is why the idea of hyphenated Canadians has always seemed bizarre to me, and why I've always been puzzled by our country's negative attitudes and misperceptions about the American "melting pot" and our own positive attitudes about the Canadian "mosaic."

As with most immigrants, my parents came for simple reasons: to find work and make a better life for their children. But my parents were coming to North America, not necessarily to Canada. For many immigrants back then, Canada was America, with little to distinguish the two.

My parents didn't choose Canada for its "mosaic" over the American "melting pot"; in fact, we would have settled in San Francisco rather than Southern Ontario if not for the death of a distant relative living there. But once here, my mother and father adapted to their new country and its customs as quickly as they could, while maintaining their Italian traditions—without any prompting from the state. Our experience wasn't unique: I suspect most immigrants couldn't care less about intellectual debates over multiculturalism so long as they're given a chance to get on with their lives in a safe and tolerant society.

All this is a long way of saying that we exaggerate the impact of public policy in determining the behaviour of immigrants here or in the United States. The notion that America forces its immigrants to give up their language, customs, and traditions is as naive as believing that Canada effectively promotes complete ethnic harmony and tolerance.

And from these myths spring others.

Another is that American immigrant kids who put their hands over their hearts and recite the pledge of allegiance grow up to be one-dimensional citizens with no connection to their pasts.

Israel Zangwell, who coined the term "melting pot" in a play of the same name in 1908, never assumed that immigrants would lose their cultural identities. Quite the contrary: not only did he think their new country would affect immigrants, he thought that they in turn would affect and influence their adopted country. In becoming Americans, immigrants from Ireland, Germany, Poland, Italy, Greece, Scotland, and parts of Asia influenced each other's customs, languages, and behaviour. In many cases, these customs were transformed to the point where they were unrecognizable in their original countries. More often than not, old-world customs would be fossilized in their new homeland to the point where new immigrants from the same countries no longer recognize them.

Many of Zangwell's observations were confirmed in Nathan Glazer and Daniel P. Moynihan's classic 1963 book on the behaviour of immigrants, *Beyond the Melting Pot*. They argued that, contrary to the early theories of assimilation, Jewish, Irish, and Italian residents of New York City never entirely shed their sense of ethnic identity—and blacks and Puerto Ricans did so even less. The book's key point is that mass culture was not destroying the old customs and distinctions of religion and ethnicity. Every ethnic group had found its own unique path to success. In his 1997 book, *We Are All Multiculturalists Now*, Glazer reconfirmed his earlier observations—even as he lamented the failure of American society to fully integrate blacks, who continue to remain far outside the cultural and social mainstream.

In 2005, Harvard political scientist Samuel P. Huntington argued in *Who Are We?: The Challenges to America's National Identity* that the United States is now undergoing a radical shift in immigration. In the past, no single foreign-born ethnic group dominated: in 1960, for instance, 1.26 million immigrants were born in Italy, followed by about one million from Germany and Canada, 830,000 from the United Kingdom, and 750,000 from Poland. By 2000, things were very different. In that year, 7.8 million new Americans (both legal and illegal) had been born in Mexico alone—followed (distantly) by 1.4 million from China, 1.2 from the Philippines, and a further million each from both India and Cuba.

This skewed level of immigration is without precedent in U.S. history. And if anyone thinks that all these Hispanics are assimilating according to some cookie-cutter melting-pot formula, they aren't paying attention. In 1990, according to the U.S. Census Bureau, 95 per cent spoke Spanish at home and 43 per cent were "linguistically isolated." And there's a strong movement, particularly in California, to promote the use of two languages to the point of creating a bilingual society. If anything, American immigrants are assimilating too slowly (or not at all)—not too quickly.

We see this trend in the growing Muslim community in the United States as well. Geneive Abdo, who wrote *Mecca and Main Street: Muslim Life in America After 9/11* (2006), challenges the notion that America's six million Muslims are well assimilated. Although Ms. Abdo found few signs of London-style radicalism among Muslims, she did find that Muslims are becoming increasingly alienated from mainstream life in the United States. Muslims in the U.S. "are choosing their Islamic identity over their American one." She goes on: "From schools to language to religion, American Muslims are becoming a people apart...." Abdo's observations are being confirmed by recent research.

A 2007 Pew Research project found that, even though a majority of Muslims in the United States are prospering more than Muslims in Europe—that is, have higher incomes—the survey also found that a significant minority are not assimilating and sympathize with radical Islam. Sixty per cent of young Muslims in the United States consider themselves Muslims first and American second. They also seem to tolerate suicide bombings as being justified. And six years after 9/11, almost half of American Muslims can't bring themselves to believe that Muslims had anything to do with it.

As Huntington has observed, there's been unwillingness on the part of many immigrants, particularly those from Arab countries, to assimilate and accept traditional notions of

American national identity. Here we aren't simply talking about outward customs or habits of newcomers such as hanging flags on rear-view mirrors, supporting their favourite soccer teams, or attending social gatherings where they play their own music, dance their dances, and frequent their restaurants. These superficial features that once passed for multiculturalism are being replaced by a fundamental rejection of American principles, values, and political systems. As Abdo concludes, "despite contemporary public opinion—or perhaps because of it—Muslim Americans consider Islam their defining characteristics, beyond any national identity." This, combined with a sense of persecution, makes for a disconcerting combination in a country where assimilation, or at least acceptance of its principles, was the defining character of a nation. This level of anti-Americanism inside the United States—by an immigrant group—is unprecedented in American history. What has happened to the traditional notion of assimilation and the American Dream?

Here Huntington blames the cultural and academic elites who promote a radical version of "multiculturalism" that he says undermines and effectively denationalizes the country. Multicultural theory, as taught in universities, asserts that assimilating immigrants is wrong, because it assumes western culture is superior. As Huntington says, "multiculturalism is basically an anti-western ideology."

Roger Kimball, editor of the *New Criterion*, in his article "Institutionalizing Our Demise: America vs. Multiculturalism," gives a compelling example of how far things have gone in denigrating western civilization. He compares the poems of

Robert Frost at the John F. Kennedy inaugural in 1961 to the one, thirty-two years later, read by Maya Angelou at the inaugural of Bill Clinton. The first referred to the heroic deeds that marked the founding of the nation in 1776, a nation that was established with God's approval and embarked on a "golden age of poetry and power." Angelou, on the other hand, saw a broken country, and she never mentions the words "America" or "American." Instead, she mentions twenty-seven racial, religious, and tribal groups and denounces the repression of these groups at the hands of the United States, accusing it of being "weeded forever to fear, yoked eternally to brutishness."

Now we learn from one of America's leading sociologists, Harvard's Robert Putnam, that the story of American ethnic tolerance may also be a myth, or at least not well understood. His recent work seems to show that ethnic groups don't show much tolerance for diversity. As reported by the *Financial Times*, "in the presence of diversity, we hunker down" and "act like turtles," says Putnam. And the lowest level of trust was found in Los Angeles, "the most diverse human habitation in human history" according to Putnam. And when adjusted for class, income, and other factors, the data revealed that the more people of different races lived together, the higher the loss of trust. Even though Professor Putnam was confident that these trends could be reversed through social reconstruction and the right policies, diversity, at least in the short run, divides communities and lowers trust. Diversity isn't the harmonious multicultural panacea many like to believe. The melting-pot view of America is a view of America that has long passed.

But let me not leave the impression that America is a seething cauldron of suspicion and racial discontent. The United States continues to be a place of promise, possibilities, and opportunity for millions of new immigrants. It is doing a much better job than European countries of integrating their immigrants. The United States just isn't the melting-pot stereotype that many Canadians believe.

Are we doing any better in Canada?

What about the Canadian mosaic myth, in which all ethnic and cultural groups remain distinct while mingling in the greater whole of a harmonious Canada? We certainly cannot mean the vertical mosaic idea presented by the Canadian sociologist John Porter, made famous in his 1965 book *The Vertical Mosaic: An Analysis of Social Class and Power in Canada*. It emphasized the inequality, both in power and income, of various ethnic and cultural groups in Canada. What I mean by mosaic is that immigrants are encouraged to maintain links to their ancestral cultures, rather than adapting to Canadian values. Isn't that what many Canadians believe? That diversity isn't the enemy of civil society, but rather its strength? That keeping ethnic groups in their boxes has made us a more tolerant society, as opposed to the American melting pot?

There is a sense from Canadian academic studies on diversity and trust that things here in Canada are different. We believe that children of immigrants, who are actively encouraged to maintain strong ties to the countries their families left behind, grow up learning to sing "O Canada" in both official languages and in the process become well-rounded citizens of the world. We have faith—a rather naive one—that those who come to our shores will magically absorb the features of tolerance and inclusiveness. We also believe that we've created a mosaic of different cultures living together in a harmonious, inclusive, and tolerant society.

If the United States isn't the melting pot most of us believe, the flipside is the myth that Canadians live in this inclusive, genteel, ethnically diverse Nirvana. The ideal of cultural pluralism is the essence of Canadian identity: some even cheer the hyphen in the hyphenated Canadian as "a bridge and not a minus sign." But in the end, such gestures signify reluctance among immigrants, a lack of commitment, and a sense of waiting to see how things turn out—hardly the best way to build a nation.

Rather than celebrating official multiculturalism, we should be trying to explain why immigrants to Canada no longer participate politically—other than being used by parties to pack local nomination meetings. Immigrants once took their civic duties seriously and quickly developed strong attachments to the institutions of the monarchy and the parliamentary system: I still have clear memories of my father and mother dressing up before going to the polls, and I doubt they ever missed a municipal, provincial, or federal election. But all that has changed.

Why are immigrants participating less? Is it apathy? Or is it that today about 75 per cent of them come from non-democratic countries with little tradition of civic participation?

Whatever the reason, we have to lay the blame partially at the feet of a government policy that places cultural pluralism above democratic traditions. The alternative argument that recent immigrants don't vote because of discrimination or alienation from a system they don't understand simply doesn't wash.

When ethnic groups do participate politically, too often they vote in blocs and on narrow issues about how Canadian foreign policy affects their homeland—a pattern consistent with broader social behaviours. When war broke out in the Balkans, tensions arose between Canadian Serbs and Croats to the point that some actually went back to fight for their counties. If we don't demand that immigrants become Canadian as quickly as possible, we can expect greater divided loyalties in the future. We must get past the notion that longstanding hostilities are abandoned the moment immigrants set foot in our country, an illusion shattered more than twenty years ago when Canadian Sikh terrorists brought down Air India Flight 182, killing 329 passengers—a tragedy with which Canadians have never come to terms.

Aside from the sheer bungling of the case by the RCMP, CSIS, and the federal government, a deeper reason for the tragedy was a belief that such a thing couldn't happen here. Because of our faith in multiculturalism, inclusiveness, and liberal principles, we assumed we were inoculated from such evil. In a political and cultural environment where ethnic communities are left completely alone, Sikh terrorists in Canada were able to intimidate, and even kill, critics in their midst, while moving freely and without fear in their community. Our concern was that we would offend if we took tougher actions against a minority group. To this day we haven't learned much. How else to explain the blatant display of a picture of one of the suspects in the Air India disaster in the April 2007 annual Vaisakhi parade—celebrating the origins of the Sikh religion—in Vancouver. The danger, in other words, is among us still, and politicians continue to blindly ignore the menace as long as there are votes to harvest.

If ethnic groups are encouraged to reject assimilation, we should not be surprised if they also bring along customs that conflict with our own. Ontario Premier Dalton McGuinty was on the verge of supporting Sharia law before it created a political firestorm in his party. But Sharia law was a natural outcome of a policy that tolerated cultural intolerance.

What's the solution? One answer is to abolish Ottawa's Ministry of State for Multiculturalism. No one would grieve except a few civil servants, academics, and assorted multicultural rent-seekers. Even Pierre Trudeau—applauded for introducing the Multicultural Act in 1971, but never wildly enthusiastic about it—would have been appalled by how it wound up segregating us. Wouldn't it be nice if we occasionally emphasized our own Canadian culture of tolerance, freedom, opportunity, and the rule of law—virtues missing in places many immigrants come from? Another solution is to educate immigrants about Canadian values of tolerance, justice, and history, important conditions before conferring citizenship.

Lazy assumptions about an American melting pot—without any attempt to understand the complexity of American society—contribute to a delusional attitude toward our own degree of success with multiculturalism. To the extent that Canada's immigrants are integrating and getting on with their lives, it's not because of multicultural social policy—it's in spite of it.

IS AMERICA THE REAL NORTH AMERICAN DEMOCRACY?

BY ANDREW COYNE

AMONG THE MANY THINGS Canadians think they know about their neighbours to the south is that their democracy is a sham. "American-style" is almost invariably a curse word in this country, and never more so than when it comes to the theory and practice of democratic government. How often have our political parties accused each other of launching "American-style attack ads"? How many times have we been warned that this or that reform will "Americanize" our institutions of government?

To be sure, there remains some uncertainty as to the precise nature of the Americans' inferiority. Is the problem with the United States that it is not democratic enough, or that it is altogether too democratic?

On the one hand, we all know the many ways in which American democracy falls short of the ideal: the overwhelming influence of big money, and the associated opportunities for conflict of interest (Halliburton and all that); the facade of competition between two parties that have very little actual differences, while behind the scenes a few rich families—what Lewis Lapham always referred to as "the oligarchy"—pull all the strings; and all summed up in the fact that fewer and fewer Americans bother to vote.

On the other hand, well, isn't there something about American politics that's just a bit ... common? More than common: unspeakably vulgar. The lack of civility in political discourse, the angry rhetoric, the deep divisions, so unlike our own peaceable kingdom. Doesn't everyone shudder at the prospect of another "circus-like" confirmation hearing for a Supreme Court judge? And what's up with all those referendums? Imagine. Letting average voters decide things. Thank goodness that sort of thing never happens here, where every issue has already been decided.

Finally, there is what our former ambassador to Washington, Frank McKenna, referred to as the "dysfunctional" U.S. Congress, hamstrung by partisan wrangling, obsessed with regional issues at the expense of a national vision, unable to look past the next election. The contrast with our own House of Commons is stunning.

So: oligarchic kleptocracy, or partisan tractor-pull? No matter. Just so long as it serves as a horrifying example.

Except that none of it is true. Well, next to none. There's a little truth in most stereotypes. But whatever the failings of "American-style" politics, they are (a) not nearly as bad as Canadians think; and (b) not necessarily worse than our own. There is as much we could learn from the Americans as teach them, and the starting point is an accurate understanding of how their system really works.

Does money talk in American politics? You bet: the same as in most democracies. The difference is that in the United

States, they've tried to do something about it. Canada recently passed legislation to ban most corporate and union donations to political parties (federal parties, at any rate; in most provinces it's still legal). Congratulations. The Americans have had similar legislation on the books since 1907.

To be sure, the parties have found and exploited loopholes over the years; hence the proliferation of political action committees (PACS) and "soft money" donations. But reformers have been just as active. The post-Watergate reforms of the 1970s limited individual donors to US$2,000. The recent McCain-Feingold bill cut that to US$1,000. Contrast that with Canada, where until very recently it was permissible for any person, corporation, or union to donate any amount they liked, to whomever they liked, with only the loosest requirements for disclosure. In the last Liberal leadership race but one—the long undeclared war to succeed Jean Chrétien—it was discovered that sitting cabinet ministers were taking huge undisclosed donations from corporate interests, in some cases from among the very industries they regulated. What penalty were they made to pay when this extraordinary conflict of interest was discovered? They had to give the money back.

Did someone say conflict of interest? Though much has been made of Dick Cheney's Halliburton connections, the fact is that he owns no shares in the company. He can't: under American law, members of cabinet must divest themselves of all their shareholdings. They have to be sold at fair market value, and to buyers with whom they are at "arm's length."

The former treasury secretary of the United States, John Snow, before he could assume the office, was required to divest himself of all of his shares in csx Corp., the Virginia railroad of which he was chief executive. Indeed, Mr. Snow sold off every other stock he owned, while outright forfeiting nearly us$15 million in csx options and other compensation to which he would have otherwise been entitled. Mr. Snow's predecessor, Paul O'Neill, was obliged to sell shares and options worth an estimated us$100 million in Alcoa, where he too had been chief executive for thirteen years. Donald Rumsfeld, the former defense secretary, was likewise required to liquidate most of his portfolio, including stocks in more than 250 publicly traded companies. Even sub-cabinet level officials, such as the White House economic policy adviser, have to divest.

Compare that to Paul Martin, who was allowed to carry on as the proprietor of Canada Steamship Lines all the while he was finance minister, even if the company was placed in a blind trust. The meaning of a "blind" trust whose contents are fully known to the holder may be debated, even had Mr. Martin not been briefed at regular intervals on the company's fortunes, and even if the company had not benefited from favourable tax and subsidy treatment—both facts that were not revealed until later. Again, the only penalty he faced was public embarrassment, and the only remedy he offered on the occasion of his becoming prime minister was to sell the company to his sons.

Had the same situation arisen in the States, it is doubtful that that would have been the end of it. While no system is immune to abuse, the institutional mechanisms for holding public officials to account in the United States are far more powerful than our own. The model of the "special prosecutor," protected by statute from political interference, has only lately been adopted here, and has yet to be tested at the federal level. Even a judicial inquiry can be shut down at the government's whim, as we learned in the Somalia affair, or stonewalled, as in the case of the Krever inquiry.

Other putative checks and balances are compromised by the prime minister's vast powers of appointment—especially a prime minister in possession of a majority. In addition to appointing every member of the cabinet, the Senate, the Supreme Court, and the federal court, he also appoints the governor of the Bank of Canada and the head of every major Crown corporation. Suppose he abuses that power—say, leans on the head of a federal bank to make a loan to a crooked friend. What is to be done? Perhaps you feel a judicial inquiry is in order. Who decides, ordinarily, whether one is to be held? The prime minister. No, you say, this is a political matter. Let Parliament look into it. But who, in a majority government, dictates whether committees hold hearings? The prime minister. Not that it would matter much if they did. Committees here have nothing like the staff or resources their congressional counterparts enjoy, and seem reluctant to employ such powers as they possess: to subpoena a witness to appear is apparently considered so rude as to rule it out in all but exceptional cases, nor are witnesses commonly required to swear an oath.

This bears some emphasis. It used to be said that a Watergate couldn't happen here: that a prime minister who was found to have done the sort of things that Richard Nixon did would be gone within days, depending as he does on the confidence of the House of Commons for his continuance in office. After the many scandals of recent years, that can no longer be said with certainty. Compare the congressional committees, with their aggressive questioning and powers of subpoena, which strike such fear into an American administration. Think of the Iran-contra hearings, or the multiple committees looking into the abuses at Abu Ghraib—and then consider the wretched efforts of the Public Accounts committee to get to the bottom of the sponsorship scandal before the prime minister, invoking yet another of his extraordinary powers, called the 2004 election.

And while we're on the subject of oligarchies: Suppose that the last three presidents of the United States, of either party, had all been from the same state, and had all once been on the payroll of the same reclusive billionaire; that one owed his considerable fortune to this connection; that another's daughter had married into the family. Would we not take this as confirmation of the dominance of the moneyed class in American life? Yet that is a description (the Kim Campbell blip aside) of our recent history, not theirs.

Oh, and that abysmal American turnout: scraping 50 per cent in recent presidential elections? Dig out our own numbers, and put them on the same basis—as a percentage of the voting-age population, rather than (as here) as a percentage of those registered to vote. It's much the same, and far worse at the provincial and municipal level. Declining voter turnout is an affliction common to most modern democracies, not a uniquely American phenomenon. And while some might see little to distinguish the Republicans from the Democrats, for sheer monotonous sameness there is nothing to compare to the almost unbroken century-long reign of the Liberal Party of Canada—or the me-tooism that was for decades the guiding philosophy of the Progressive Conservative Party. The existence of the New Democratic Party, often held up as an example of our ideological heterogeneity, in fact bespeaks the opposite. The Co-operative Commonwealth Federation, its progenitor, was born of the left's inability to make inroads in either of the two main parties during the Depression—whereas in the United States these found expression in the Democratic Party of Franklin Delano Roosevelt.

In fact, today's Republicans and Democrats differ sharply on many points: over Iraq, over social security, over taxes and health care, and any number of other issues. They appear alike only through the same distorting lens that sees a vast gulf separating Americans' attitudes from Canadians'—that is, from the perspective of the Canadian left. Canadians are neither so liberal, nor Americans so conservative, as their respective caricatures would suggest. It's just that in the United States the actual divisions that exist within any society are allowed to play out, whereas here they are suppressed. Opinion on gay marriage, for example, often cited as a point of distinction between the two countries, divides very nearly on the same lines in both, especially if the two outliers—Quebec and the South—are left out.

Is that the real problem, then? That there's too much democracy in America—that personal attacks and unvarnished opinions flourish, while civilized debate languishes? There's no doubt that American political campaigns have a certain, um, robustness, and certainly American talk radio regularly tests the limits of free speech. But let's not overstate things. Harsh as "American-style" campaigns may be, no American candidate for president has ever campaigned, as the Liberals did in 1988, on the theme that "my opponent is in league with foreign interests to sell out the country." Nor is there anything to compare to the sort of free-for-all our televised debates have become, with every candidate shouting over the other. In the 2000 presidential debates, Al Gore lost points for sighing too loudly.

In the most basic and literal sense, however, it is true that America is a more democratic society than ours—for good or ill. A much wider array of offices is open to election, including sheriffs and judges in some states, with more institutions of government to elect them to, given the separation of executive and legislative branches and the prevalence of bicameral legislatures. Politics is a more pervasive part of life in some ways. You are expected to register as a Democrat or Republican, for example, and vote in organized party primaries, rather than the kind of fevered buying and selling of memberships that decides nomination races in this country. The whole House of Representatives and a third of the Senate are elected every two years; presidential election campaigns, it seems, now overlap, the next beginning before the last has finished. And yes, there are all those referendums—hundreds of them, every election cycle.

But what's wrong with that? Referendums are hardly unknown in this country, and there is persuasive evidence that they make for better government, resolving divisive issues in ways that are accepted on all sides and providing an important check on the pretensions of legislators. The American legislative process, likewise, may be cumbersome and time-consuming, but much more of it is done out in the open, and there are more opportunities for public input. It may take, for example, nine months or more to pass a budget through both houses of Congress. But are we so sure of the superiority of doing things the Canadian way: with a lockup, a speech, and a few days of perfunctory debate? Congressional representatives may have more power to buck the party line, even to trade their votes. But do we really prefer the rows of trained seals that Parliament has become? Need we even mention the disgrace of the Canadian Senate, the patronage house (sometimes known as "the taskless thanks"), appointed for life and resisting to this day every effort at reform?

Much of the popular revulsion so easily aroused against any proposal to "Americanize" our system is based, not just on sweeping generalizations about the American system (Supreme Court confirmation hearings, for example, rarely degrade into the sort of "circus" we are constantly warned against—that's why the ones that do gain such notoriety) or ignorance of our own (the behind-the-scenes machinations that have traditionally accompanied Supreme Court appointments in this country mean our system is just as "politicized," in its own way), but on an instinctive attachment to the status quo.

Just because something is the case now does not mean it must always be—or that it always was. Perhaps the biggest myth about American democracy is that it is indeed "American-style": that their commitment to it is unique, reflecting some innate difference between us and them. But it was not ever thus. The historian Christopher Moore, in *1867: How the Fathers Made a Deal*, argues that Confederation-era Canada was one of the most democratic societies on earth. Upper Canada, certainly, had much the same grassroots, town-hall ethos as the New England states, and for much the same reason: an economy based on small, roughly equal landholdings. Members of Parliament were held closely to account by their ridings, and lived in fear of being thrown out of office, neither party affiliation nor incumbency being quite such guarantors of success as today.

This tradition died slowly. It was the convention until well into the twentieth century, for example, that appointees to cabinet resign their seats and seek the approval of their electors in a by-election, their role having changed from that of watchdog on the executive (even as members of the governing party) to members of it. It wasn't terribly practical—governments were defeated on more than one occasion after their cabinets, fresh from appointment, resigned en masse, thereby depriving them of their majorities—but you have to love the spirit of it.

Moore traces much of the decline since then to the innovation, adopted at the Liberal Party convention of 1919, of electing party leaders at large, by a vote of all the member of the party. Until then it had been the prerogative of the parliamentary caucus, as in the classical Westminster model. Although this sounds less democratic, in practice it had the effect of keeping party leaders on a much tighter leash; as their position at all times depended on the approval of the members they led in Parliament, they tended to be much more solicitous of their concerns. Compare that to the present system, where a leader, emboldened by the vote of the party, may use and abuse the caucus as he pleases, answering only to the occasional "review" by the membership, in which he is routinely confirmed with majorities of 90 per cent or more.

What a long way we have come. For all the desire of the Fathers of Confederation to avoid the "excesses" of American democracy, we were much more like them at our founding than we are now. Yet we remain much more like them now than we like to admit, and would do well in some respects to emulate them further.

BRED IN THE BONE

BY ROBERT FULFORD

SAUL BELLOW, WHO WAS BORN IN LACHINE, Quebec, and moved with his family to Chicago when he was nine, retained a rueful sympathy for his country of birth long after he emerged as a profoundly and explicitly American author.

The narrator of the title piece in his 1984 collection, *Him with His Foot in His Mouth and Other Stories*, points out that it's not easy to share a border with the United States. As he explains, "Canada's chief entertainment—it has no choice—is to watch (from a gorgeous setting) what happens in our country . . . there is no other show. Night after night they sit in darkness and watch us on the lighted screen."

It's probably safe to say that no Canadian has ever put such a pathetic construction on Canada's cultural relations with the United States, but Bellow's account contains a painful element of truth. There are times when geography threatens to make us a nation of spectators, pressing our noses against the glass of the border, while history unfolds beyond our reach.

This situation raises deep and uncomfortable questions about our national life. How have we played the cards that fate has dealt us? How should we confront this inescapable fact of our national life?

Answering those questions has frustrated us for generations.

It may be that formulating intelligent, imaginative answers is beyond our powers. In any case, we have so far thought of nothing better to do than create a politics of envy and develop our own particularly nasty strain of anti-Americanism, a pathology that imposes a crabbed, limited view of both Americans and Canadians. While it touches everything we do, we articulate it most vividly within the world that Ottawa has taught us to call "the cultural industries."

A powerful mythology came to dominate Canadian thinking about the arts early in the twentieth century. It was so appealing, so rich in pathos and in the opportunities it presented for self-pity, that it became the principal narrative of Canadian culture. In this legend, the United States appears as a crushing force, the permanent enemy of the Canadian spirit, so pervasive that it cripples us; it always has and perhaps always will, unless we make the most strenuous efforts to defend ourselves.

By mid-century, that conviction was strong enough to infect the central document in the history of Canadian cultural politics, the 1951 report of the Royal Commission on the Arts, Letters and Sciences, chaired by Vincent Massey. Unlike many royal-commission reports, Massey's was a huge success. Almost immediately, it began flowing through the bloodstream of the country. It put us permanently on the defensive.

Throughout his life, particularly during his years at Oxford and his service as Canada's high commissioner in London, Massey's sympathies lay mainly with England. When the Massey report was written, much of the culture of English-speaking Canada was dominated by English immigrants, but that was a version of alien influence that Massey didn't mention and probably didn't notice. The United States was both bad example and menace. England was an inspiration.

The report encouraged the federal government to create the Canada Council, support CBC television, and otherwise invest in developing culture and mass communications. But it also set in stone an official approach to U.S.-Canada cultural relations that encouraged Canadians to see themselves beset by the barbarians to the south. It led to negative and nationalistic attitudes.

The Massey report argued that Canada had to fear both the benign influence of the United States (big foundations giving grants to Canadian institutions, thereby blunting Canadian initiative and impeding independent growth) and the malign influence (mass culture saturating Canada, turning Canadians into copies of Americans).

As a Toronto anglophile, Massey seems to have known little of American mass culture, except that its popularity threatened to destroy the possibility of a distinctive Canada. To fight it we would have to inject public money into the arts.

This led naturally to the belief that arts institutions, and the arts themselves, were not of value for their own qualities but existed principally as dikes holding back the ocean of Americanization that threatened to drown us. Partly because of Massey's report, we have been haunted ever since by that vision. It injected political concerns into every aspect of the arts.

George Grant, later the author of a highly popular anti-American tract, *Lament for a Nation* (1965), contributed a paper on philosophy to the Massey Commission in which he condemned the United States as "a barbaric empire which puts its faith in salvation by the machine." Grant was slowly developing a critique of modern institutions and modern life; he saw rejecting America as essential to the rejection of modernity. His later work amounted to an emphatic rejection of the technological society that was accepted as normal in the West.

Certain impressionable readers of Grant took up his views without quite understanding their implications. The young radicals who read Grant in the 1960s were not indebted, as he was, to the anti-modern philosophy of Martin Heidegger. Unlike Grant, they never realized that in disliking America, they were also expressing a dislike of themselves and their own lives. Equating the American system with inhumane capitalism (standard practice on the CBC and in the universities) became the Canadian way of enjoying the fruits of the technology-dominated world while pretending we have no responsibility for them.

This attitude of imaginary innocence, a habit of distancing ourselves from whatever we believe we should abhor, shows up even in the most minor aspects of culture. A few years ago the *Globe and Mail* ran a heading over John Doyle's TV column: "The empty inanity of American celebrity." In another piece, Doyle described watching TV on "a dull day of mind-numbing American piffle-culture." Hard as it is to accept, what we call American mass culture should be called North American mass culture. Many Canadians help to make it, often as stars or producers. Canadians form a willing part of the audience for it. Yet many among us, such as Doyle, believe we can refuse to share responsibility for it, as if "American piffle-culture" were not carried on Canadian TV and watched by millions of Canadians.

It's as if we consider ourselves duty-bound to argue against Americanization while simultaneously embracing it. Several years after Starbucks became a national institution in the United States, it still hadn't opened a single coffee house in Toronto. So *Toronto Life* magazine published a message: "Starbucks, come already" (eventually, Starbucks did). This was a typically Canadian complaint: the editors couldn't bear to be left out of a major American fad. And of course, after Starbucks did arrive, its presence was described as another fateful step on the road to Americanization.

The mythology propagated by Massey and thousands of successors produces a kind of patriotism that's sour and resentful. A defensive posture may occasionally be necessary, but as a long-running policy it's self-defeating. It distorts the self-image of Canadians and perverts our institutions. In many cases it provides a convenient excuse for failure.

It has so coloured opinion in English-speaking Canada that, in many circles today, it is considered eccentric not to express reflexive anti-American views, along with contempt for the American president and his administration. On the CBC a vigorous pro-American opinion sounds outrageous and certainly upsets faithful listeners. CBC producers ensure that such opinions are seldom heard. A CBC friend of mine defines anti-Americanism as the CBC's "default position"—it's the assumption from which programs begin and, usually, end.

Describing the effects of this pathology in a newspaper piece two years ago, I said that it does little harm to

Americans, who mainly fail to notice it. I now realize I was quite wrong. I heard from many American readers who had been subjected to anti-Americanism and were not amused.

A letter from an American-born professor at the University of Western Ontario was typical: "I must say that I, and my American friends here, are very sensitive to it but seldom say anything about it, because doing so would have so little effect on those who are engaging in it. We never tell a Canadian (including neighbours) that we are Americans unless we absolutely have to. It just makes life a little easier for us and our children." He reported that anti-Americanism has become far more pervasive than it was when he arrived in Canada in 1966. It seemed to him that it grew alongside multiculturalism: "There has to be a dark background in order to highlight the virtuous cultures; and we are that dark background."

Anti-Americanism spreads happiness among those to whom it seems both natural and virtuous. It spreads a warm, satisfying feeling among certain Canadians and encourages delusions of superiority. It also provides a polite and acceptable form of bigotry. People who would die of shame before tolerating homophobia, racism, or anti-Semitism will cheerfully join in denunciations of Americans.

A few Americans promised to leave the United States for Canada if George W. Bush were re-elected in 2004. That prompted Nora Jacobson, an American medical sociologist living in Toronto, to write a post-election article in the *Washington Post* under the heading "Before You Flee to Canada, Can We Talk?" She reported that "In 'officially multicultural Canada,' hostility toward Americans is the last socially acceptable expression of bigotry and xenophobia. It would be impossible to say the things about any other nationality that Canadians routinely say—both publicly and privately—about Americans."

Anti-Americanism also (and this is not a small point) prevents us from using U.S. accomplishments as examples to be emulated. The late Frank Underhill, a great teacher and an enemy of anti-Americanism all his life, made this point when reviewing the Massey Commission report in the *Canadian Forum*. He wrote that Canadians should be seeking, not avoiding, closer contact with the finest expressions of the American mind. "The fear that what will result from such contact will be our own absorption is pure defeatism."

Today we might take one instance among many: the problem of explaining science to the general public. In this crucial form of journalism you could never say that the Americans are better than the Canadians; the distance between the two countries is so great that a comparison would be inherently preposterous. Yet science journalists in this country, so far as I can tell, have learned nothing from their American contemporaries.

Our book publishers, movie producers, and others spend their time worrying about American power when they should be worrying about the quality of whatever they are preparing to offer the Canadian public. The fear of American hegemony serves as the intellectual framework for the legions of bureaucrats who work in the arts councils, the department of communications, and the many arts organizations. They look to the fear of America as justification for their careers, while judging every idea on how well it defends Canada—or "saves" Canada, as they often put it.

Jean-François Revel, French writer and philosopher, once said that, if anti-Americanism were suddenly removed from French politics, France would have no political thought at all. Much the same could be said of Canada. Anti-Americanism provides the one issue that unifies Canadians and the one set of comfortable arguments we can insert into the discussion of every subject, from trade to health care and from culture to defence. If you knew nothing about Canada except its political rhetoric, and ignored the actual lives of the citizens, you might well conclude that anti-Americanism gives Canada a reason to exist.

Anti-Americanism also functions, for demagogues, as a reservoir of apparent virtue. Using it, they can depict themselves as saviours of their nation. In the period from 1957 to 1963, Prime Minister John Diefenbaker made a career of it; in the 1990s and the first years of this century, Prime Minister Jean Chrétien was still using it as a button he could always push when his image as a hero needed boosting. At a 1997 NATO meeting in Madrid, he was overheard saying that, whenever possible, he did what the Americans didn't want him to do. "I make it my policy," he said. "It's popular."

In many Canadian minds, the struggle with the United States plays out on the field of values, cultural and political. Each country has certain values, and Canadians appear to have decided that ours are superior.

We more closely resemble Americans than any other people on earth, yet in our public and private discussions we make an elaborate show of rejecting American ideals. In an individual this might be considered a sign of mental illness, or at least a dangerous form of self-deception. As a way of thinking in public, it gives our relations with the Americans an unreal, even hallucinatory, quality. It also limits any chance we might have to develop as a mature and independent society. Those who judge themselves against the Americans are dominated by the Americans, whether they admit it or not.

We could place the blame for our confusion at the feet of Prime Minister Wilfrid Laurier, who unintentionally led us toward a national fantasy of independence. He negotiated a reciprocity treaty with the United States but failed to convince Canadian voters that they would benefit from it. In the 1911 election they rejected Laurier and the treaty, perhaps hoping to expand their traditional relationship with Britain. The people said "No" to economic integration with America, and the people were obeyed—or so our history books told us. In class we all learned that, in trade matters, 1911 was a key election.

That was true in the schoolroom, and perhaps in a few university courses, but nowhere else. Outside school, we were surrounded by American cars, American magazines and books, American literature, and American thinking. We dressed like Americans, listened mainly to American music, watched mainly American movies, and gazed at American television. American fads usually became our fads, American technology our technology.

And, for the most part, American values became our values. How could they not? Like the Americans, we are a continent-wide pluralist democracy founded by Europeans and later modified by successive waves of immigration. Like the Americans, we shape and express our shared attitudes through

mass culture. There are differences (such as government support for Roman Catholic schools in parts of Canada and the
open participation of fundamentalist Christians in U.S. politics), but in general we work from the same assumptions
because we have roughly the same hopes and problems.

So the great rejection of 1911 was no rejection at all. I can't
remember anyone in a history class pointing out this flagrant
discrepancy between what we said and what we did. Had we
inquired, we might have learned that, over a few decades,
Prime Minister Mackenzie King slowly drew Canada toward
the relationship that his mentor Laurier had envisioned.

King learned from the political failure of 1911. He spoke
quietly and carried a small stick. He did everything in bits and
pieces, especially trade with the United States. He avoided
dangerous words, such as "reciprocity" and "free trade." Still,
he gradually lowered the barriers between the two countries,
making each change appear either inevitable or so minor that
it could be called a purely technical adjustment, certainly
nothing to bother the voters about. King preferred that the
citizens think nothing much was happening, and the citizens
went along with it.

All the while, the fears of the anti-Reciprocity campaigners
leaked into the stream of ideas directing the country's cultural
life; and in turn the attitudes of artists and other cultural figures affected the discussion of trade. When the Free Trade
Agreement became the focus of the 1988 federal election,
what Canadians had begun calling "the cultural community"
turned out to be its most ferocious critics. Artists and broad-
casters who had never before expressed interest in non-tariff

trade barriers suddenly became experts on the dangers of free trade. Two clusters of opinion, one political and one cultural, not often connected in previous eras, formed an alliance. They agreed that Canada was endangered, culture was endangered, even health care was endangered. In the next nineteen years, there was little evidence that the agreement had produced negative results, and much evidence that it had made the country richer.

That argument over free trade, largely pointless as it turned out, can stand permanently as a spectacular case of anti-Americanism put to crass political use. Members of the Liberal Party who remember it probably consider their leader's hysterical rhetoric of 1988 as nothing more than a political gimmick that didn't quite work. But surely it left a powerful residue of anti-U.S. feeling.

Is there a shelf-life for anti-Americanism? On a TV program, I heard someone raise the possibility that, if the United States made major changes, anti-Americanism would disappear. What if Americans withdrew their troops from foreign countries, agreed to put all their activities under UN direction, and used the money saved on armaments to build the world's finest all-inclusive national health-care plan?

What would happen to anti-Americanism then? How would we still feel superior? Robbed of the sustenance provided by American military action and the lack of American health care, anti-Americanism (the argument goes), would wither and die.

On the contrary, it would find new sources of nourishment. After all, we had anti-Americanism long before we had a national health program, and we had it in those distant times when the Americans were the great stay-at-homes of world politics, condemned in many countries for their isolationism—condemned especially by many Canadians for coming late to both the First and Second World Wars. Finding reasons to dislike them was never hard. They were always richer than we were, for one thing, and they misused the English language. Schoolteachers and other common scolds warned the young against "Americanisms," such as "swell," long before the emergence of the American sins we now criticize. "Vulgar Americanism" was a phrase often used in the 1950s by the general manager of the Canadian Press news agency in memoranda condemning examples of careless language used by his reporters or editors. Besides, the Americans bragged too much and spoke too loudly. They were provincial—not cosmopolitan, like us. Worst of all, many of them really didn't know we existed, or care.

It seems unlikely to me that anyone now living will see the end of self-blinding anti-Americanism. It is bred in the bone of Canadians. But possibly some future generation will find a way to stop worrying and appreciate the Americans for what they are. Should that happen we may discover that we can also appreciate ourselves for what we are.

THE FUTURE OF CANADA–U.S. RELATIONS: BRING BACK THE SPECIAL RELATIONSHIP

BY ALLAN GOTLIEB

FOR THE BETTER PART OF A CENTURY, our history shows that every Canadian prime minister has faced two supreme challenges in governing our huge and diverse land. One is maintaining national unity, especially as regards the place of Quebec and French Canada in Confederation; the second is managing the relationship with our giant neighbour, which just happens to have by far the world's largest economy and happens to be the world's supreme superpower.

The history of managing our relationship in the post–Second World War era can be divided into broad periods—four in all. The first, for want of a better term, is the period of continentalism and the special relationship; the second is the period of attempted diversification away from continentalism and North American exceptionalism; and the third is the period of constructing a more rules-based and institutionalized framework for conducting our relations.

We are now in the fourth era, in which much of our effort to address border and regulatory issues with the United States is being conducted in a trilateral context, with Mexico being the third partner. One might possibly say that we are now in the era of trilateralism. But it might more accurately be described as a decade and a half of drift.

It is easy to be nostalgic about the past, but it is not an exaggeration to say that, for a couple of decades after the Second World War, Canada and the United States enjoyed "the golden period" of our relationship. As the British Empire waned and our colonial ties weakened, and as the Cold War developed and the western powers faced the greatest geopolitical challenge of the second part of the century, Canada, under the leadership of William Lyon Mackenzie King and Louis St. Laurent, pursued a foreign policy based on the realities of geography. Our economic relations and investment patterns shifted overwhelmingly from Britain to the United States, and our North American defence relationship deepened through production-sharing and a variety of defence-related agreements.

This was also an era of close collaboration between Ottawa and Washington in multilateral institution building. Because of closely shared values, both of us looked at the world in a very similar fashion and worked together to resist threats to peace, security, and freedom. Canada made enormously heavy defence expenditures—as high as 40 per cent of the federal budget in the mid-1950s—and was an architect of NATO, and a close Western collaborator in the fight against Soviet expansion.

In spite of the remarkable growth of the economic relationship between our two countries, we managed it with surprisingly few bilateral institutions. With the exception of the International Joint Commission, the Permanent Joint Board on Defense (PJBD), and NORAD, and a short-lived attempt at establishing joint Cabinet committees between our two governments, what developed into the world's closest and deepest two-way relationship was governed by ad hoc methods. "Ad hocery" was the hallmark of the era.

But "ad hocery" could not have worked so smoothly and effectively without the belief that the relationship between the two countries was special.

The record shows that the United States, on a number of occasions, was willing to subordinate its economic interests (as it perceived them) to the larger purpose of maintaining good relations with Canada. It seems at times that it was the policy of the United States not "to treat Canada like any other foreign government." There are documents that testify to this.

There were many reasons for this. In the Cold War, Canada's northern "real estate" was seen as especially significant from a geopolitical standpoint, given our ownership of the land mass separating the two superpowers. Hence U.S. strategic interests could be understood as virtually dictating special consideration for Canada. Even more significantly, there was a sense of trust and friendship. For example, when the United States considered nominees for the post of first Secretary General of the United Nations, two Canadian civil servants topped the list: Lester Pearson and Norman Robertson.

There were a number of occasions when excessive protection for U.S. economic interests was seen as not compatible with U.S. strategic interests. Hence, Canadian oil imports into the United States were granted an overland exemption from restrictions on foreign imports of oil into the country.

In this same period, when President Kennedy imposed an Interest Equalization Tax on investment abroad, the special relationship meant that, when Canada protested, once again we got an exemption. The United States on some occasions refrained from applying its pernicious extraterritorial laws on trading with the enemy to our trade with China in trucks and machinery.

When serious countervailing-duty issues arose as a result of duty-remission schemes for the manufacture of automobiles in Canada, it was the United States that proposed to Canada that we consider an automotive agreement for tariff-free trade between our two countries in the automotive sector. It then used its power and influence to help obtain GATT approval. Thus, in 1965, the Auto Pact was born.

In 1971, when the Nixon administration and its Secretary of the Treasury, John Connolly, imposed a surcharge on all imports into the United States in order to address its unfavourable balance of payment (the famous "Nixon Shokku"), Canadian protests were once again heard, and the surcharges for Canadian imports into the U.S. were lifted.

It was no accident that the period of the special relationship corresponded closely with the period of the Imperial Presidency: The Congressional role was distinctly subordinate to the Administration. Moreover, the powers of Congress were exercised in a disciplined way by the dominant Congressional leaders.

Nothing better illustrates the relationship of the time—and the changes that were soon to take place—than the memoirs of Arnold Heeney, who was our ambassador to Washington twice during these years. Heeney wrote that he did not have to deal with economic issues in his time. They were not on his agenda. Nor did he lobby the Congress. Nor did any Canadian ambassador do so until decades later. We followed the rules by the book: the Congress, being an internal organ of the government, was off limits.

On one occasion some senators from the Midwest were sponsoring a bill that would have caused a diversion of the waters of the Great Lakes, to Canada's great detriment. Heeney went to the State Department to complain, in accordance with traditional diplomatic practice. The senior State Department official told him he could do nothing.

"Complain to the Congress," he told him.

"Who should I see?" the ambassador asked.

"Lyndon Johnson, the Senate majority leader," was the reply.

"Will you make the appointment?" Heeney asked.

"Yes," was the response.

Heeney made the call, told Johnson that he had a problem, and explained it. Johnson then said, "No boy, you don't have a problem."

"What do you mean?" said Heeney. "I just explained it."

Replied Johnson, "And I just fixed it."

In the Trudeau years, however, deep forces were at work that brought about a fundamental change in Canada's approach to dealings with the United States. In Canada, widespread disillusionment arose about the war in Vietnam and U.S. global leadership. In the United States, there was growing anxiety about a perceived decline in its economic primacy. At the same time, a growing confidence was emerging in Canada about our own global role and pride in our achievements as a middle-power at the U.N.

In the Nixon–Kissinger era of détente, there was also a sense that the threats of the Cold War were receding and the need for solidarity with allies was diminishing. Among our elites, the conviction grew that we needed to assert more vigorously our independence from the Americans on the global stage.

Astonishingly, at the beginning of the Trudeau government, relations with the United States were ignored in its major foreign-policy review, *Foreign Policy for Canadians*; but a few years later, it published its celebrated or notorious (depending on your point of view) *Third Option*. The point of the policies advanced in that document was to reduce our dependency on Uncle Sam—and in particular to reverse the trend towards continental integration.

The document advocated that Canada diversify our trade, especially with Europe and the new financial superpower, Japan, through contractual links. Beyond that, in a newly nationalistic mood, the *Third Option* proposed that Canada strengthen the domestic instruments of our national economy through greater ownership and control of our national resources.

Accordingly, the Trudeau government introduced foreign-ownership policies (FIRA) and national-energy policies (Petro Canada, National Energy Policy) aimed, again, at asserting our independence on the global stage and reducing our dependence on the United States.

With this change of direction, it was inevitable that the

very notion of a "special relationship" was deemed inappropriate and fell from favour.

The Trudeau policy initiative was unfortunate, first in its timing and second in its underlying assumptions.

As to timing, it failed to take account of deep and important political changes underway in the United States. We proclaimed our view that special consideration for our interests was no longer necessary at the very moment when we were going to need it more, i.e., when Congress was reasserting its jurisdictional primacy in the area of external trade.

Ottawa was out of touch with the revolution in governance that was taking place in Washington in the wake of the Vietnam War and the Watergate fiasco. As the Presidency was weakened, so was party discipline. A new crop of younger post-Watergate Congressmen came to Washington, eager to exert power and influence.

Decision-making in Congress became fragmented and atomized as the spectre of protectionism cast a giant shadow over its corridors. Trade Acts were passed giving U.S. regulatory bodies far-reaching powers to investigate and retaliate against perceived discrimination against U.S. goods and services. Sections 201 and 301 actions and anti-dumping and countervails mushroomed to the point where almost nothing that came from under the ground or grew on top of it or moved in the sea escaped attack.

Thanks to legislative initiatives in Congress, buy-America actions, and procedural trade remedies, the hit list included lumber, hogs, beef, cod, uranium, steel, wheat, berries, rolling stock, and manufactured products of various sorts.

FIRA and the NEP stoked the political fires and gave rise to an outbreak of retaliatory threats and actions.

Because of the weakened presidency and the fear of decline in U.S. industrial primacy, the era was now over when the United States would subordinate its economic interests to its geopolitical goals. Prominent senators, such as the eminent senior Democrat Lloyd Bentsen, trumpeted this fact to foreign audiences, just in case America's trading partners were not getting the message.

Meanwhile the Trudeau government was coming to realize that diversification of our trade was not happening. The opposite was true—during the years following the promulgation of the *Third Option*, our exports to the United States rose from some 60 per cent of our total exports to around 80 per cent. That was the state of things when Trudeau finally took his walk in the woods in the winter of 1984.

Even the Trudeau government was beginning to realize this hard reality. In its final years, it tried to negotiate sectoral free-trade agreements with the United States but these went nowhere. Too little and too late.

By the time of the Liberal government's defeat in 1984, Canadian policy vis-à-vis the United States was at an impasse. There was no special relationship to offer any political safe harbour from the protectionist storms of the era.

Breaking with the past, the Mulroney government ushered in the third era in the management of our relationship. Although not originally in favour of a comprehensive free-trade agreement with the United States, the Mulroney government changed gears within a year or so of its election.

The free-trade proposal that was advanced by Canada had several ground-breaking features.

a) The Canada–U.S. free-trade zone was to be bilateral in nature. On a one-on-one basis, we were seeking a closer economic embrace from our much-feared neighbour to the south. Ottawa did not have a more extended North American or Western hemisphere agreement in mind. It was a preferential regime between Canada and the United States;

b) It was to include all sectors of the economy, with the exception of culture. That meant investment, services, energy, and other resources;

c) Trade remedies were to be abolished or restrained;

d) New institutional arrangements were to be entered into to settle disputes—the first innovative proposal in the institutional field in half a century or more of our bilateral relations.

What Prime Minister Mulroney proposed was a more secure, rules-based legal regime to support the phenomenal flows of trade and economic activity between our two countries.

Despite the degree of hostility in the Congress (at one time approximately forty senators were opposed to the accord) and weak leadership on the part of the administration, our goals were largely achieved. The result was a major increase in the free flow of goods, services, and people across our boundaries with exports tripling in scale. Moreover, in spite of the horrendous softwood-lumber dispute, there has been a significant falling off in the number of U.S. trade actions initiated against Canadian exports.

The adoption of a rules-based approach by the Mulroney government constituted a rejection of the idea of the "ordinariness" of the Canada–U.S. relationship. Because, in the Free Trade Agreement, the countries granted preferential status to each other, it restored the notion that Canada and the United States enjoyed a special relationship, and the Free Trade Agreement built on that fact.

But the evolution of North American free trade since that time revealed that there were problems in going further in the direction of integration.

First, the Canada–U.S. Free Trade Agreement soon evolved into a trilateral accord, the North American Free Trade Agreement, or NAFTA, in which Mexico shares a privileged market access position into the United States. Canada lost its unique status. But the problems and challenges in the Mexican–U.S. relationship were very different from ours.

Second, as was recognized at the time, the Free Trade Agreement, though it accomplished much in furthering a rules-based relationship, fell short of what needed to be attained. There were no agreed-upon rules in the critical area of what constitutes a subsidy, there were serious weaknesses, as time was to show, in the dispute-settlement provisions, and much work needed to be done to embrace unfettered free trade in such areas as agriculture and forest products and to facilitate the free movement of peoples across boundaries.

But thirdly, neither the Canada–U.S. Free Trade Agreement

nor its successor NAFTA contained within them the dynamic necessary to lead to its own improvement. There were no mechanisms to spur momentum towards deepening and widening the common economic space our countries were building.

Moreover, the two Liberal prime ministers who succeeded Mulroney, Jean Chrétien and Paul Martin, deliberately did not seek to build upon the newly reinvigorated special relationship forged in the previous decade.

Once again, differentiation and distance resumed their primary place in Canadian foreign policy, at the expense of the national interest.

At the same time, over-reliance began to be placed on lobbying Congress and on exercises in public relations.

The consequences for Canada would not have been so serious had the events of September 11, 2001, not taken place. The effect was transformative. National security soared to the top of the U.S. agenda to an unprecedented degree, and an era was born in which defence of the homeland trumped all other concerns. New obstacles began to arise impeding cross-border commerce and the movement of peoples. In other words, the Canada–U.S. border began to thicken. Some even referred to its "Mexicanization."

The Chrétien government struggled to address the issues—with some success—through its "smart border" negotiations with the United States in the wake of 9/11. In time, this effort evolved into the much broader trilateral process launched in Waco, Texas, the Security and Prosperity Initiative, through which the three North American states sought to address the vast array of regulatory and security obstacles that stood in the way of the further deepening of our common economic space.

The effort continues to this day. Judging by what is happening—or not happening—at our borders, the process seems to be moving very slowly. It has lacked the leadership, energy, and momentum necessary to achieve results. Now, thanks to the congressionally-inspired Western Hemispheric Travel Initiative, with its requirement for overland passport controls, Canada and the United State are at risk of reversing the great historic trend towards reducing the significance of the border in our national life.

The opportunity should have been taken, after the destruction by terrorists of the World Trade Center, to pursue a grand initiative to create a single economic and security space, with a common security perimeter, which allowed the free movement of our trade, services, and people across the northern border. The deep integration of our two economies required special recognition of the uniqueness of our relationship.

Whether such an agreement could have been attained is debatable. But arguably, U.S. security interests and Canadian economic concerns provided the constituent elements for trying to construct a grand bargain of sorts. A decade and a half ago, great skepticism existed as to whether a Canada–U.S. Free Trade Agreement could have been attained in the increasingly protectionist environment of the United States. This time we decided not to try.

Where do we stand in the current state of our relationship with the United States?

With a minority government in Canada and a lame-duck administration in the United States, heavily preoccupied with Iraq, this is not, admittedly, the most propitious time for grand initiatives or possibly even for modest ones.

But, on the other hand, the relationship between Ottawa and Washington has significantly improved since the election of Stephen Harper's government. Moreover, our formidable commitment to fight terrorism in Afghanistan has substantially increased goodwill towards Canada, both in the White House and on the Hill, and among both Republicans and Democrats.

Why not propose to the United States that we begin to explore ways to advance our respective national interests through greater recognition of the special nature of our relationship?

Canada and the U.S. could:

1. Commit to convene official annual summits between the president and the prime minister. These began in the Mulroney-Reagan years and were highly productive. But the practice seems to have lapsed. Summits of this nature increase dramatically the focus and priority which Canadian issues would receive at the highest echelons of the U.S. system.

2. Establish special procedures for the preparation of these summits and their agenda, under the control and direction of the two leaders.

3. Reinstitute the commitment to hold quarterly meetings of our foreign minister and the U.S. secretary of state, established in the Reagan years, but unfortunately also allowed to lapse. This was a unique

feature of U.S. diplomatic practice, due in part to the initiative of George Shultz. It guaranteed "quality time" for top officials to get their counterparts to focus on their grievances and concerns. Structure it so as to allow other ministers to participate.

4. Adopt the same practice for ministers in other key areas—e.g., energy, the environment, and law enforcement.

5. Develop a protocol between our two governments, at the direction of our two leaders, for better managing the relationship. Such a protocol could define principles for cooperation, for example, that prior notification and opportunity for consultation would be provided by each country to the other, with regard to any initiative that could have an adverse impact on the other's interests—whether economic, environmental, or security-based.

Given the way the U.S. Congressional system operates, and the fact that, as with the Western Hemispheric Travel Initiative, so many of our problems originate in the Congress, obtaining such an agreement would be very meaningful for Canada. Admittedly, such a commitment, which is to be found in the Free Trade Agreement in incipient and limited form, will not be easily arrived at. But it would also be of substantial benefit to the United States (think legalization of marijuana).

6. Appoint personal envoys, or czars, answerable directly to the president and prime minister, to

take hold of the entire process of border facilitation and provide direct, top-down leadership.

7. Establish the principle that new bilateral institutions should be created to plan, maintain, and oversee the openness and smooth functioning of our borders. Vast economic consequences hinge on how well they are managed. Unilateral decision-making in management, regulation, and infrastructure planning affecting the principal choke points should be brought under the responsibility of new transborder commissions with effective powers to deal with the issues at hand.

There is a whiff—more than a whiff—of the nineteenth century in how we currently go about our business of border management. Take the international bridge at Buffalo/Fort Erie as an example. Years pass and the problems of congestion, insufficient infrastructure, and security remain unresolved. Too many players, too many jurisdictions, too little planning, too much unilateralism.

Almost a century ago, the International Joint Commission was formed by Britain and the United States to manage issues relating to our international boundary waters. A century later, our approach to management of the land frontiers remains mired in obsolete notions of sovereignty.

8. Set up a ministerial-led task force or special envoys, answerable to the president and prime minister, with a mandate to begin planning for

the negotiation of a new comprehensive agreement to create a single economic and security space embracing our two countries. This should include extending the scope of the existing Free Trade Agreement, adopting a common external tariff, rules of origin, and customs union, strengthening dispute-settlement procedures, restricting or abolishing trade remedies, establishing a common security perimeter, and furthering the free movement of people across our boundaries. Could such an agreement be obtained? Only with patience and great difficulty. But free-trade experience shows that in the Congress big initiatives can have a greater chance of success than small ones. (More interests in play, more trade-offs available, more opportunities for national interests to trump local ones.)

9. Be willing to privilege the bilateral route when it is to our advantage. As with NAFTA, the template that our two countries establish would be available to Mexico or others.

Canada is in a special relationship with the United States. We should recognize it, build on it, and be proud of it.

"YOU WANT AN AMERICANIZATION OF CANADIAN HEALTH CARE!"

BY DAVID GRATZER

IT'S A SCENE THAT REPLAYS ITSELF over and over again—a discussion about health reform with two learned experts. The conversation shifts from provincial initiatives, to aging demographics, and then over to insider observations. One will voice his idea that more profound change is needed; the other suggests that this would amount to an "Americanization" of Canadian health care.

It's a charge that resonates, because people look at the U.S. system as too free-market, too expensive, and too inefficient. The suggestion that the idea of reform may push medicare down the road to an American-style system is, thus, devastating. Canadians are afraid of the system next door, and I understand—not that long ago, I too subscribed to these beliefs. Indeed, it seems wasteful to dedicate a chapter considering American health care. If there is one topic Canadians think they know, this is it—it's a near obsession on the part of our political class.

But after careful study, I've come to a different conclusion: I believe that practically nothing said or written about the American system is, in fact, true. And I'll go further: The basic problems of Canadian and American health-care systems are similar. Until we appreciate the similarities, we cannot properly reform medicare.

———

I am an accidental health-policy wonk.

Growing up in Canada, I didn't spend much time contemplating the nuances of health economics. I wanted to get into medical school. My mind was filled with statistics on MCAT scores and admission rates, not health spending and GDP percentages.

As a Canadian, there were three things I soaked up from my environment: a love of ice hockey, an ability to convert Celsius into Fahrenheit in my head, and the belief that government-run health care was compassionate. If I was fully confident in our system north of the forty-ninth parallel, American health care seemed to me absolutely unappealing: the high expense, the tragedy of the uninsured, the dissatisfaction. When HillaryCare was debated in Washington, a city I had never visited, I remember thinking that they were on to something.

Gradually, my own views on Canadian health care changed. The most important lesson I learned wasn't in the classroom, but on the way to one. On a blisteringly cold Winnipeg morning, I decided to cut through the hospital ER in order to shave a few minutes off my commute. Swinging open the door, I stepped into a nightmare: the ER was packed with elderly people on stretchers, awaiting admission. Some had waited five days. The air hung heavy with the odours of sweat and urine and fear. At that moment, I began to reconsider everything I thought I knew about Canadian—and American—health care.

What I discovered was a health-care system in which ERS were routinely and dangerously overcrowded. And the problems weren't confined to just one area. Patients waited for practically any diagnostic test or procedure. The stories were numerous and pathetic: the man with ongoing pain from a hernia repair, whom we referred to a pain clinic with a three-year waiting list; the woman in need of a sleep study to diagnose what seemed like sleep apnea, who faced a two-year wait; a woman with breast cancer, who was asked to wait four months for radiation therapy when the standard of care was four weeks.

I wrote about what I saw, and my articles were published in a handful of newspapers. Frustrated by the limitations of seven-hundred-word essays, I decided to push further, and so—with no training in health policy and no background in writing—I decided to write a book. By day, I attended classes and did rounds of patients; at night, I worked on my manuscript. The end result was my first book on health care, *Code Blue*.

If I re-examined my views on our system while working on *Code Blue*, it was impossible for me not to take a second look at the system in the United States. To my surprise, despite the seemingly endless negative commentary on U.S. health care in Canada, much of everything that I had heard about their system proved false. What struck me when I was doing my research was the extent to which experts would excuse the inexcusable in Canada—waiting lists and the like—because of their fears of the American system.

Almost a decade has passed since *Code Blue* was published. Yet, in so many ways, the world of Canadian health policy remains bipolar: you either accept our system or you are charged with pining for the cruel world of the American one. The point is brought home literally as I am writing this essay. Belinda Stronach, Liberal member of parliament, went to the United States for part of her cancer care. In a letter to the editor, a Toronto physician explains that, while Stronach might have been hypocritical in her actions, Canadians still don't want American-style health care. I can think of no other public policy debate that carries such a burden of national identity—and, tragically, of so much nonsense.

Nonsense is a strong word, but I chose it deliberately. So much of what is said about the American system just isn't true.

Let's consider some commonly accepted "truths."

Forty-seven Million Americans Lack Health Care

The number forty-seven million is accepted as an irrefutable fact in political stump speeches, Hollywood movies, and Robin Cook novels.

But the forty-seven million statistic is an estimate, and it creates, in the words of Douglas Holtz-Eakin, former director of the Congressional Budget Office, "an incomplete and potentially misleading picture." The figure is drawn from the Current Population Survey, conducted by the Bureau of the Census for the Bureau of Labor Statistics, after surveying fifty thousand households. It's a thorough tool, but hardly without shortcomings. Not surprisingly, other surveys—like the Medical

Expenditure Panel Survey (MEPS) and the Survey of Income and Program Participation (SIPP)—have arrived at different estimates. When the Congressional Budget Office studied the issue in 2003, they found a range of statistics on the uninsured:

- 21 to 31 million Americans were uninsured for the entire year;
- 39 to 42.6 million Americans were uninsured at any point in time;
- 56.8 to 59 million people were uninsured at some time during the year.

Why the inconsistency? The problem isn't just in the differences among the studies, it's also in the subject itself. The number of uninsured Americans is constantly changing, making estimates of the size of this population a moving target. David Henderson, who served as health economist for President Reagan's Council of Economic Advisers, explains:

> Many people believe that the forty-seven million uninsured people in the United States are the same people, year-in, year-out. That belief is false. Imagine that Eastman Kodak invented a camera that could take a collective picture of those forty-seven million people and still show the detail of each person's face. Let's say the camera takes a picture of those people and then takes a picture five months later of the forty-seven million people who are without health insurance.

Question: What percentage of the people in the first photo are also in the later photo? Answer: About 50 per cent. In other words, fully half of the people who lack health insurance at a given time have health insurance just five months later.

Why is insurance non-coverage so transient? Because most jobs in the United States carry health insurance for those employees who want it, and because many of the non-insured are people who are out of work. Unemployment is short-term for most people—the median duration of unemployment in 1998 was seven weeks—so going without health insurance is also short term. Both the Census Bureau and the CBO note the transient nature of non-insurance. The CBO also calculated the duration of spells of non-insurance, and found that 84 per cent of the uninsured are without coverage for less than twenty-four months.

But numbers aren't everything. Many argue that, even if the forty-seven-million statistic is misleading, the problem is real. The uninsured are depicted in popular culture as lost and forgotten (picture the single mother in the emergency room, struggling to make ends meet for her three children). But the uninsured are a heterogeneous group.

Drawing on Census Bureau data, the Blue Cross and Blue Shield Association found in a 2003 report that a third of the uninsured have family incomes of more than $50,000 a year, and for 16 per cent of the uninsured, incomes exceed $75,000 a year. A Health Affairs study on non-poor uninsured Californians pegs their average annual health spending at $200 per person. Many people have done the math and have decided not to get coverage. In addition, a third of the uninsured already qualify for Medicaid or some other type of program. Of the remaining third, many are without insurance for only a brief period, usually less than a year. To be sure, there are eight million Americans who slip through the cracks, unable to get coverage. But that's far fewer than the commonly quoted disaster figure of forty-seven million.

Canadian Health Care Outperforms the American System

Canadian experts often like to cite statistics on life expectancy and other health outcomes, concluding that Canadians get better value for their health dollars.

And, yes, America lags behind other countries in crude health outcomes. But such outcomes reflect a mosaic of factors, such as diet, lifestyle, drug use, and cultural values. It hurts me as a doctor to say this, but health care is just one factor in health. Americans live 75.3 years on average, fewer than Canadians (77.3) or the French (76.6) or the citizens of any Western European nation save Portugal. Health care influences life expectancy, of course. But a life can end because of a murder, a fall, or a car accident.

Such factors aren't academic—homicide rates in the United States are much higher than in other countries (eight times higher than in France, for instance). In *The Business of Health*, Robert Ohsfeldt and John Schneider factor out intentional and unintentional injuries from life-expectancy statistics and find that Americans who don't die in car crashes or homicides outlive people in any other Western country.

And if we measure a health-care system by how well it

serves its sick citizens, American medicine excels. Five-year cancer-survival rates bear this out. For leukemia, the American survival rate is almost 50 percent; the European rate is just 35 percent and the Canadian rate somewhere in between.

The U.S. System Is a Free Market

American health care has become synonymous in the minds of Canadian commentators with a radical, free-market-type of health care.

But government plays a major role in health care south of the border. Consider these basic spending statistics: for every dollar spent on health care in the United States, roughly forty-seven cents comes from government coffers. Public programs that help individuals are numerous: Medicare (for the elderly), Medicaid (for the poor and disabled), SCHIP (for children), and VA (for veterans). The government system is so vast that it covers all elderly Americans, a third of all childbirths, and roughly half of long-term care.

Let's put this in perspective: on a per capita basis, the United States spends more on government health care than does Canada.

What's most striking about a study of American health care, though, is the extent to which government influences the private health-care sector. Take, as an example, the regulation of insurance. Many Americans buy their own health insurance (though most are covered by a public plan or a policy purchased for them by their employer). And from a distance, you'd think that Americans had a relatively free hand to choose an insurance policy if they wanted to do so. Yet individual states have highly regulated the market, meaning that even the most basic policies must cover certain procedures (like IVF therapy) or certain providers (like nutritionists).

In 1965, only seven benefits were mandated by the states; in 2004, according to the Council for Affordable Health Insurance, there are 1,823. The list includes: acupuncturists (in 11 states), chiropodists (3), chiropractors (47), denturists (2), marriage therapists (4), massage therapists (4), osteopaths (24), and social workers (28). Some states also mandate that specific services be covered: birthing centres with midwives (6), breast reconstruction (48), clinical trials (19), dental anaesthesia (27), hair prostheses (7), IV fertilization (15), maternity stay (50), off-label drug use (37), second surgical opinions (11), and TMJ (temporomandibular joint) disorders (19). These regulations have an impact—a basic family policy in New Jersey costs a family of four more than the lease of a new Ferrari.

Here is the central point: American health care is the most heavily regulated sector in that economy. There are so many regulations and tax rules that American health care has much in common with its Canadian counterpart.

———

On both sides of the forty-ninth parallel, people fret about rising health costs. This decade, those costs have risen sharply. Health-insurance premiums have roughly doubled between 2000 and 2005 in the United States; in Canada, provincial health budgets rocketed some 50 per cent during that time—more modest than American increases, but vastly out-pacing inflation, nonetheless.

Many health-care experts see rising health-care costs as an inevitable and unavoidable consequence of advances in medical science. Medicine is better than ever, so it seems only reasonable that we pay more for this excellence.

And no one can question that medicine is better than ever. Consider the health of the vice president of the United States. Mr. Cheney has endured four heart attacks—and yet he is not only able to rise out of bed and walk up a flight of stairs, he holds full-time employment. A short time ago, that would have been unthinkable: people often died of their first (and last) heart attack. Mr. Cheney, of course, isn't the only one to benefit from these advances. Death by cardiovascular disease has fallen by two-thirds over the last sixty years. That sort of progress is seen throughout the medical field: childhood leukemia, once a death sentence, is curable; polio is confined to the history books; depression, once a quiet plague, is now treatable.

The irony is that in most other sectors of the economy costs fall with advancements in technology. Think of unit prices (the computer on your desk is vastly superior to its predecessor ten years ago, yet costs a fraction of the price) or spending as a percentage of GDP (we spend less on agriculture, yet food is more plentiful). But the advancement of medical science has, curiously, not followed the trend; progress has begotten greater expense.

Why then is health care so different from other sectors of the economy? Simply put, because of the curious manner in which we have organized health care. Perhaps most surprisingly,

Canadian and American health-care systems are very similar in this regard.

As I write in my most recent book, *The Cure*, two days define health care on this continent: December 1, 1942, and October 26, 1943.

On December 1, 1942, Lord Beveridge issued his report on health care and pensions to the British parliament, envisioning zero-dollar public health insurance. Lord Beveridge had enormous influence in Canada; his thinking (and persuasiveness) helped lay the intellectual foundation for medicare. We still maintain his core idea: there are no user fees or deductibles in Canada.

On October 26, 1943, the IRS ruled that American employers could continue to pay health-insurance premiums in pre-tax dollars. As a response to wage and price controls, employers had begun to offer health benefits to attract better employees. The IRS ruling legitimized and encouraged the practice, giving rise to the dominance of employer-sponsored health insurance in the United States. Jump ahead more than six decades, and the majority of Americans are receiving their health coverage through their workplace. And, because this is paid in pre-tax dollars, the insurance tends to cover a great deal: everything from emergency treatment to annual physicals to basic blood tests.

At first glance, the resulting health-care systems couldn't be more different. Americans obtain their insurance from their employers. They speak of benefits, contributions, and co-pays. Canadians, in contrast, are covered by their government; the jargon is full of words like medicare and coverage. Yet, from an economic point of view, Americans and Canadians—albeit for different reasons—pay pennies on the health-care dollar. That is, the end result of Beveridge's report and the IRS ruling is that Americans and Canadians—whether privately insured or publicly covered—tend to be over-insured, and thus less sensitive to prices.

With Americans and Canadians paying just pennies out of pocket for every health dollar, they have little incentive to economize on health expenses. In fact, we seem collectively ignorant of the most basic prices in health care. Ask a Canadian or American friend how much it costs to go to his family doctor with a common cold, and he or she will stare blankly at you.

But with rising costs, policymakers on both sides of the border have been faced with containing costs. In Canada, the solution has been simple enough: rationed care. Canadians, as mentioned, are resigned to wait for practically any diagnostic test or surgical procedure. According to the government's own statistics, 1.2 million Canadians are actively looking for a family doctor, but can't find one. Patients in Ontario can only dream of having the access to PET scans that are available to lab animals enrolled in research studies. With growing frustration, governments all over the country are pouring new money into the social program.

Across the border, managed care was the seductive idea of the 1970s and 1980s. If people had no incentive to economize, then corporate bureaucrats, armed with statistical tables and endless zeal, would do that for them. With the collapse of the managed-care gambit in the late 1990s, health costs continue to soar in the United States.

"YOU WANT AN AMERICANIZATION
OF CANADIAN HEALTH CARE!"

Which leads us back to the common problem faced by policymakers on both sides of the border: how to deal with health inflation. The answer is not as illusive as it may seem. We simply need to accept that our 1940s model of health care doesn't work in an age of PET scanners and intrauterine surgery. Canadians and Americans are frustrated by bureaucrats making decisions for them—whether it be government bureaucrats (here) or corporate bureaucrats (there)—and thus we need to move decisions closer to individuals.

That is, after all, the way we've organized the rest of the economy. And in health care, it would be a prescription for lower costs and higher quality. First things first, though: we need to end our obsession with the virtues of our system over that of the Americans.

ACROSS THE
MEDICINE LINE

BY TOM FLANAGAN

"The experience of all the dead generations weighs
like a nightmare on the brain of the living."
—Karl Marx, *The Eighteenth Brumaire of
Louis Bonaparte* (1852).

UNLIKE HEALTH-CARE INSURANCE, peacekeeping, and other topics
discussed in this volume, the treatment of aboriginal people is
not something on which contemporary Canadians pride themselves in comparison to the United States. Rather, the dominant
view seems to be that "Eurocanadians" have committed terrible
injustices against native people, for which compensation is now
due. But in the nineteenth century, Canadians lauded themselves on the Crown's treatment of native people, contrasting
the peaceful settlement of Canada with the Indian wars mark-
ing the expansion of the American frontier.

There are indeed some important differences (as well as
even more important similarities) between the American and
Canadian treatment of native people, and to understand them
requires an excursion into history. Mindful of an old academic
joke (An anxious student in a history seminar gives his first
presentation and then asks the professor, "How did I do?"

"You need to give more background," replies the prof. So the student begins his second presentation by saying, "Slowly the earth cooled ...."). I will not go back to the cooling of the earth, but some background is necessary here.

What is now eastern Canada was originally settled by the French, who simply proclaimed the sovereignty of France without recognizing any aboriginal title to the land. That led to fierce Indian wars in the seventeenth century, especially with the Iroquois; but the French did not occupy a great deal of land except around the Bay of Fundy and in the Saint Lawrence valley. The fur trade proved to be more lucrative than farming, and that required treating Indians as allies and business partners rather than as an impediment to settlement. In contrast, the mainly agricultural British colonists to the south recognized the concept of Indian title to the soil and often attempted to purchase land rather than simply seize it. But disagreements were inevitable, and frontier wars erupted over land issues.

Geography proved to have far more impact than legal theory upon Indian-white relations. In Canada, the Precambrian Shield creates a daunting barrier between the fertile soil of southern Ontario and the agricultural lands of the western prairies, so there could be no spontaneously moving agricultural frontier. In the United States, in contrast, there is no real barrier to settlement from the Appalachian Mountains to the Rocky Mountains, between which lie the immensely fertile lands of the American Midwest and South. Once pioneers got through the Appalachians, which happened by the middle of the eighteenth century, no force in the world could have held up the flow of westward settlement.

King George III and his advisers did, in fact, try to turn back that tide. After acquiring the French territories in North America through the Treaty of Paris, they released the Royal Proclamation of 1763, which reserved the land west of the Appalachians as "Hunting Grounds" for "the several Nations or Tribes of Indians, with whom We are connected, and who live under Our Protection." They were not to "be molested or disturbed in the Possession of such Parts of Our Dominions and Territories as, not having been ceded to, or purchased by us, are reserved to them." Any white men living in the Indian country were called upon "forthwith to remove themselves." Because "great Frauds and Abuses have been committed in the purchasing Lands of the Indians," the Proclamation forbade any further purchases by private persons. However, "if, at any Time, any of the said Indians should be inclined to dispose of the said lands, the same shall be purchased only for Us, in Our Name, at some publick Meeting or Assembly of the said Indians to be held for that Purpose by the Governor or Commander in Chief of Our Colonies respectively, within which they shall lie."

Far from effectively protecting Indian lands from further encroachment, the Proclamation became one of the causes of the American Revolution; and once the Northwest Territory passed from British to American sovereignty, settlement proceeded quickly and inexorably. The pattern was much the same in most of the United States. Outrunning effective government control, land-hungry settlers would move into Indian country, wars would erupt, and the defeated Indians would sign a new treaty, ceding ancestral lands and moving farther west. In a tragedy comparable to the expulsion of the Acadians, the United States even deported the Cherokee Indians from the Appalachian states across the Mississippi River.

As a result of these frontier wars and deportations, there are no Indians in most of the eastern United States, except for individuals who have moved back in more recent times. Original Indian communities managed to persist only in Maine, upper New York State, Florida, and northern Michigan and Wisconsin, while a few submerged bands, heavily intermarried with white and black Americans, have recently reappeared in states such as Massachusetts, Connecticut, and North Carolina. This is truly a sad part of America's past, and Canadians can be justifiably proud that nothing similar happened in their history. After 1763, the only violence on the Canadian frontier took place in the North-West Rebellion of 1885, in which a few Indian bands got involved, though it started as a Métis uprising (Métis have never had any form of legal recognition as a separate people in the United States, which remains another enduring difference from Canada).

Given the facts of Canadian geography, agricultural settlement did not easily outrun government control. Much of Canada remained a fur-trading preserve of the Hudson's Bay Company until late in the nineteenth century, so native people continued to be indispensable business partners, living much as they always had. Where agriculture was possible, representatives of the Crown negotiated land-surrender agreements before, not after, the influx of settlers. Guided by the American experience, Canadian authorities deliberately dealt not with whole tribes or nations but with small bands of

Indians, granting numerous but dispersed reserves to make it harder for the Indians to offer any resistance. The Canadian approach to treaty-making proved to be a practical way of taking control of the land while avoiding bloodshed and allowing native people to remain in (an admittedly much reduced part of) their ancestral territories.

This was the model in Ontario and the three prairie provinces. In Newfoundland, though, the original inhabitants—the Beothuk—were exterminated. The pattern in the other Atlantic provinces and Quebec was essentially similar to that in Maine and New York State—settlement on Indian reserves after episodic warfare, without formal land surrenders. Very few treaties were signed in British Columbia; there, most Indians were confined to reserves by legislative fiat. And nineteenth-century treaty-making did not extend to the Yukon and Northwest Territories because there was as yet no pressure for agricultural settlement.

Yet after this long period of difference between the United States and at least part of Canada, Indian policy converged closely in the two countries. When the era of treaty-making finished, the emphasis switched to civilizing the Indian. In both countries, this meant keeping native people in paternalistic tutelage on reserves while pursuing three policies: encouraging the work of Christian missionaries; educating Indian children, using residential schools as a major, though not the only, means of instruction; and promoting agriculture by furnishing instructors, seed grain and livestock, and farm machinery.

The main difference between Canada and the United States in this period (the late nineteenth and early twentieth centuries) was the passage south of the border of the General Allotment Act (Dawes Act) in 1887. This legislation, which remained in effect until 1934, resulted in much reserve land being deeded to individual Indians and often resold to outside purchasers. As a result, most Indian reservations in the western United States are legal checkerboards, with some lands owned by the tribe and others owned by individuals, both Indians and non-Indians.

In these years, Canadian Indian reserves were also diminished, though in a more governmentally controlled way. Bands surrendered surplus land to the Department of Indian Affairs, which then sold the land to private purchasers and used the proceeds for the improvement of the reserves. Over a period of decades, hundreds or even thousands of these surrenders took place, giving rise to the large number of "Specific Claims" currently under negotiation in Canada.

After the Second World War, the paternalism of Indian policy began to change in the United States and Canada— slowly at first, then with gathering speed in the wake of the Civil Rights movement of the 1960s. Features common to both countries include:

- Cleaning up unfinished business by negotiating surrenders for unceded lands. Americans accomplished this with the Alaska land-claims settlement of 1971. Negotiating modern treaties is a much bigger challenge in Canada because it includes at least the Northwest Territories, Yukon, British Columbia, northern Quebec, and Labrador, whereas in the United States it involved only Alaska;

- Reducing the control of the Indian Affairs bureaucracy and emphasizing self-government at the band or tribal level;
- Shutting down residential schools in favour of local schools in Indian communities;
- Trying to promote economic development on Indian reserves as a way of increasing standards of living.

Although the thrust of modern policy is much the same on both sides of the border, the more left-wing flavour of contemporary Canadian political culture has created some visible differences. For one thing, there is more emphasis in Canada on symbolic appeasement. Thus the word "Indian" has virtually disappeared from public discourse, except where it has to be used in legal discussions of the Indian Act, to be replaced by the tendentious neologism "First Nation," whereas Indians are still Indians in the United States.

There has also been more emphasis in Canada on compensation for real or alleged historical injustices. Thus the federal government not only closed residential schools but offered $2 billion in compensatory payments to survivors of those schools. Also, the Specific Claims process allows bands to challenge the validity of land surrenders that took place decades or centuries ago and to receive monetary compensation for their loss. Based on awards made to date, it could cost $10 billion or more to deal with hundreds of as-yet unsatisfied claims. In the United States, there has been no compensation for residential school survivors, and the government has not offered to pay anything for reserve lands lost through the operation of the Dawes Act, let alone through warfare.

Canada has also tried to deal with aboriginal issues at the constitutional level. Clauses on aboriginal and treaty rights were inserted into the Constitution Act of 1982 (Charter of Rights and Freedoms), thus giving constitutional status to both old and new treaties; Brian Mulroney appointed a Royal Commission on Aboriginal Peoples, many of whose recommendations amounted to constitutional amendments; and there were numerous provisions dealing with aboriginal peoples in the failed Charlottetown Accord of 1992. There has been no parallel movement to constitutionalize native issues in the United States, where Indians remain subject to the paramount sovereignty of Congress.

Does all this mean that Canada now treats "its" Indians "better" than the United States does? The answer depends on what is meant by "better." While the United States has not dealt as much as Canada in symbolic and constitutional gestures and in compensation for historical injustices, it has been more innovative in some down-to-earth ways. One example is casino gambling on Indian reservations, which received legislative authorization from Congress in 1988, making some American Indians, most notably the Pequots of Foxwoods, Connecticut, fabulously wealthy. Casino gambling has subsequently come to Canadian Indian reserves, but more slowly and on a smaller scale. Another example is the Harvard Project on American Indian Economic Development, founded in 1987 and supported by the Ford Foundation. Researchers from the Harvard Project have been invited by many reservations to study their institutions of tribal government with the aim of making them more conducive to economic progress in a capitalist society. There is simply nothing comparable in Canada, where aboriginal economic development remains largely the domain of federal policy, without a boost from prestigious civil-society organizations.

These differences in aboriginal policy between Canada and the United States reflect larger differences in contemporary political culture. Canadians seem to place more emphasis on the public sector—symbolic appeasement, constitutional entrenchment, and compensation for past injustices—whereas Americans seem to look beyond government to entrepreneurship and civil society. These differences are interesting, but how important are they in the greater scheme of things? In comparing two countries as similar as Canada and the United States, we should be wary of the narcissism of small differences. In fact, when we look at the big picture, the contemporary status of aboriginal people in Canada and the United States seems much the same:

- Aboriginal people are small minorities in both countries—about 1 to 2 per cent of the population in the United States and 3 to 4 per cent in Canada. The variety of definitions used makes it hard to be more precise.
- The assimilation of aboriginal people is irreversible in both countries. Aboriginal languages are dead or dying, replaced for most purposes by English. Aboriginal people wear the same clothing, eat the

same foods, and pursue the same recreations as other North Americans. There are sub-cultural variations, but that is true of many ethnic minorities.

- In both countries, aboriginal people have lost most of their original land base, but still own large amounts of land—certainly more land per capita than the rest of the population. Much of this territory is remote or even wasteland, but it is potentially valuable for recreation, tourism, and resource extraction. However, the property-rights structure (public ownership, with the federal government as trustee) is cumbersome and makes it hard to extract full economic value from the land.

- When statistical averages are computed, aboriginal people are at or near the bottom of the economic hierarchy in both countries. They trail most other ethnic groups badly in terms of income, longevity, health indicators, and social pathologies.

- There is enormous variation among aboriginal people in both Canada and the United States. Particularly on reserves and reservations, many live in poverty reminiscent of Third World conditions. Yet there are also many successful aboriginal entrepreneurs, as well as an ever-growing aboriginal middle class of educated professionals and managers.

Canadians can be proud that their history of relations with aboriginal peoples was more peaceful than that of the United

States in the nineteenth century. But that advantage flowed more from the facts of geography than from moral superiority. And in any case, it seems to have made little difference in determining the present-day state of affairs, which is remarkably similar on both sides of the Medicine Line.

The challenge, as clearly described in Jared Diamond's best-selling book *Guns, Germs, and Steel*, is the encounter of societies that are effectively thousands of years apart in terms of historical development. The native inhabitants of North America were themselves quite differentiated, ranging from hunter-gatherers organized in small bands to relatively sophisticated chiefdoms, such as the agricultural Cherokee and Iroquois of the east and the salmon-fishing tribes of the Pacific Northwest; but all must be classed as Neolithic. None had metallurgy, literacy, or the state form of social organization; nor did they have resistance to the infectious crowd diseases brought by the European newcomers. The Neolithic cultures of North American Indians resembled those of the inhabitants of Europe five thousand years earlier, yet they had to confront expeditions sent by the most advanced nations of Western Europe.

Both Canadians and Americans recognized Indians as rational human beings, similar in principle to themselves. Some may have agreed with General Sheridan that "the only good Indian is a dead Indian," but extermination or enslavement of Indians was never the policy of either country. Both sought to civilize Indians, to teach them the virtues of Christianity, European-style intensive agriculture, private property, literacy, and formalized government. Reserves and reservations were not supposed to be permanent enclaves of otherness, but temporary shelters in which native people would be protected while they learned the arts of civilization. But such vast programs of cultural transformation are more easily projected than carried out. What was initially thought likely to take perhaps a generation or two has now stretched out over centuries, with no end in sight.

There have indeed been some successes. Indians have been converted to Christianity, have largely given up their ancestral languages for English, and have embraced literacy and formal education. Some have thrived in the new environment and become successful businessmen, professionals, athletes, entertainers, and politicians. But others have been left behind, living on government charity in squalid reserves or urban ghettoes. Where cultural change has failed, at least part of the explanation is the continuing influence of Neolithic cultural norms that were adaptive in their original setting but are counterproductive in a modern society. Tribalism restricts contacts with outsiders that could lead to economic progress. Close affiliation with family and kin hampers the individualism required to succeed in education and employment. The rhythm of Neolithic life, alternating intensive hunting and gathering with periods of leisure, is at odds with steady application leading to success in modern societies.

In short, both Canada and the United States set out to do the same thing, to incorporate Neolithic peoples into dynamic modern societies. Measured against their aspirations, neither has succeeded fully. Cultural change is always difficult, particularly in constitutional governments where it is generally assumed that culture is a spontaneous part of civil society rather than a product of public policy. Nonetheless, there are those on both the Left and the Right who dream of sweeping new approaches to aboriginal issues.

The Left fantasizes about aboriginal self-government. But in reality aboriginal communities are small and economically dependent on the societies in which they are now embedded. Municipal-style self-government is a real and desirable possibility, but full-fledged sovereignty is simply not going to happen. Nor would the millions of aboriginal people on both sides of the border who are already well assimilated into the larger society even want it to happen.

The Right fantasizes about doing away with special status altogether—abrogating treaties, repealing legislation that gives aboriginal people special rights, privatizing the reserves and reservations, letting Indians be simply one more ethnic group in a pluralistic society. This also is not going to happen. Treaties, reserved lands, and special legislation are anchored in hundreds of years of history and will not be simply swept away. They are defended by powerful vested interests— hundreds of band or tribal governments, as well as national organizations of native people. In Canada, moreover, the whole system is now constitutionally entrenched, so that Parliament can change almost nothing without getting prior agreement from native people themselves.

Inertia is the dominant fact of the aboriginal situation, and no grand scheme capable of changing it has any chance of being legislated in either country. Public policy, then, should be occupied with trying to make improvements at the margin. On reserve, that ought to mean more flexible property rights, more accountable and transparent local government, and better education for new generations. Off reserve, the dynamism of the North American market economy and open society offers enormous opportunities to those willing and able to participate in it. But just as both Canada and the United States have programs to help immigrants adjust to their new home, native people may need that kind of help as they move from remote rural locations to cities and towns in search of a better life. Such a course of "benign neglect," as Daniel Patrick Moynihan once proposed for African Americans, lacks the inspirational quality of grand visions, but it may satisfy the cardinal precept of good medicine and good public policy: "First, do no harm."

THE ENVIRONMENTAL QUESTION

BY NEIL REYNOLDS

As CONDESCENDING AS IT SOUNDED, this sanctimonious homily—delivered in the midst of a federal election campaign—was implicitly meant to distinguish Canada (as a morally superior country) from the United States (as a morally inferior country). A prime minister doesn't denigrate another country by accident. Thus Liberal Prime Minister Paul Martin's calculated *cri de cœur* at the celebrated Montreal conference on climate change and the Kyoto Protocol in December 2005: "To the reticent nations, including the United States, I say that there is such a thing as a global conscience and now is the time to listen to it."

Although Canadian prime ministers have famously lectured the United States from time to time, this was the first time that a Canadian prime minister had done so as an oracle for Gaia. Mr. Martin presumably aspired to multiple tactical gains with his allusion to the earth goddess—distinguishing Canada from the United States, distinguishing himself from U.S. president George W. Bush (and, as a kindred conservative, from Conservative leader Stephen Harper). By evoking the global eco-conscience, Mr. Martin sought to define the election as a simple choice between the Liberal good and the Conservative evil.

It didn't work. In January 2006, Canadians gave Mr. Harper a minority government and ignominiously ended Mr. Martin's political career. Gaia, it turned out, was a jealous goddess. Mr. Martin had especially ticked off the NDP and its holier-than-thou leader, Jack Layton. How dare Mr. Martin speak for the global conscience, Mr. Layton thundered, when Canada's greenhouse gas emissions—"if you can believe it"—had increased at a faster rate under Liberal leadership than they had increased "in George Bush's United States." Mr. Layton doesn't speak anti-American slurs. He spits them.

And Mr. Layton had a point. Mr. Martin had neglected to mention that Canada's GHG emissions had increased by 24.4 per cent in the eight years of Liberal government since 114 countries adopted the Kyoto Protocol—eight years in which U.S. emissions had increased by only 12.8 per cent. Odd, isn't it, how people who feign moral superiority so frequently trip on their own pretenses? One week after Mr. Martin's epiphany at Montreal, in a nationally televised leaders' debate, Mr. Layton hurled the technically precise word— "hypocrisy"—at the prime minister. It stuck.

Though always risky, hypocrisy is commonplace in politics. When former U.S. president Bill Clinton attended the same conference in Montreal, he spoke critically of Mr. Bush's refusal to support the Kyoto Accord—but neglected to mention that GHG emissions were increasing at a much slower rate in the U.S. during Mr. Bush's presidency than they had during his own. When former U.S. vice president Al Gore visited Toronto a year later, he declared that the world was looking to Canada for "moral leadership" on the environment—but neglected to mention that the Clinton-Gore administration had never tried, in eight years, for Senate approval of the Kyoto Protocol.

More ironic still, none of these champions of the global conscience deigned to acknowledge that it's the maligned Mr. Bush who may well go down in history as the first president to preside over an actual decline in GHG emissions in the most carbon-intensive economy on earth. Whether Mr. Bush deserves personal credit for this milestone or not, he has the same right to claim it as does any president or prime minister who serendipitously times his years in power with historic achievements.

Will this GHG "tipping point" occur during the presidency of Mr. Bush? In its 2007 analysis of leading environmental indicators, the San Francisco–based Pacific Research Institute says that the breakthrough moment is imminent. When the final numbers for 2006 and 2007 are calculated, the think tank said, they will probably show that U.S. carbon emissions have declined in absolute terms for the first time ever in a non-recessionary economy—"the first time that greenhouse gas intensity has improved at a faster rate than economic growth."

Gaia will presumably be pleased, regardless of Mr. Bush's conservatism. Significantly, the transformation will have happened without the help of the Kyoto Protocol, signed personally by Mr. Gore in 1998 but never submitted to the U.S. Senate for ratification—for the simple reason that the Senate would never have ratified it. (In 1997, the Senate indicated unequivocally—in a stunningly bipartisan 95–0 vote—that it would not accept any GHG treaty that exempted developing countries.) In the end, in any event, the responses of Canada and the United States to the Kyoto Protocol were identical. Both countries signed it; neither did anything to implement it.

Simply put, though, Americans have nothing much to learn from Canada in the area of environmental protection. As wealthy countries, Canada and the United States, along with affluent European countries, have made significant commitments to the environment—and have cleaner air and purer water to prove it. As befits rich countries, they will spend progressively more in the future. When parts per million have been managed, they will invest in parts per billion; when parts per billion have been managed, they will invest in parts per trillion. Among all of them, though, statistical differences will remain, reflecting different priorities in different neighbourhoods.

Generally speaking, when Canada performs better than the United States, it is because we have fewer people. When the United States performs better than Canada, it is because the U.S. has tougher environmental regulations—the "stringency test"—and because it spends more money. For the next clean-up of the Great Lakes, for example, the United States has committed US$2 billion; Canada has committed $40 million.

On energy efficiency, however, the United States performs far better than Canada, Mr. Martin and Mr. Layton notwithstanding. In their 2006 Environmental Performance Index (EPI), for example, Yale University and Columbia University say that Canada needs 14,227 terajoules of energy to produce US$1 million in GDP; the United States requires only 9,112 terajoules. (It is not necessary here to know the meaning of terajoule; only that *tera* means monster.)

There are good reasons for the difference but the gap is quite astonishing—given the Canadian pretense of moral superiority. On the other hand, the Yale–Columbia EPI says that Canadian air quality is superior (measuring 56.2 on a scale from 1 to 100), well ahead of U.S. air (which measures 44.7). By these numbers, Canada's air is 25 per cent cleaner than U.S. air.

The Yale–Columbia EPI says that the U.S. performs better than Canada on another high-priority environmental indicator: sustainable energy. Again using a scale that runs from 1 to 100, the U.S. scores 69.7; Canada scores 62.8. And the United States performs better than Canada in preserving biodiversity and habitat: the U.S. scores 66.9; Canada, 56.2. Yet, on a comprehensive comparison that Yale–Columbia labels as "environmental health," the two countries get almost identical marks—as common sense would suggest: U.S., 98.3; Canada, 98.6. Good scores. Yet the Yale–Columbia EPI, as with almost all such ranking exercises, puts Canada ahead of the United States. Go figure.

These global rankings, however, have produced such improbable conclusions that someone needed independently to rank the rankings. In 2004, Environment Canada commissioned a scholarly study to determine what these inexplicable calculations really meant. Researchers Rose-Marie Petersen and Paul R. Samson examined six ranking reports:

- The Yale–Columbia Environmental Performance Index, cited above, which ranked Canada sixth out of twenty-three countries (and the U.S. fourteenth).

- The Yale–Columbia Sustainability Index, a companion report, which ranked Canada fourth out of 142 countries (and the U.S. eighteenth).
- The Ecosystem Wellbeing of Nations Index (EWI), a British report, which ranked Canada as third (and the U.S. fourteenth). It was the EWI, incidentally, that famously ranked the Republic of the Congo as the number one country in the world.
- The Friends of the Earth's Revised Environmental Sustainability Index, which ranks Canada forty-second in the world (and the U.S. 112th). In this ranking, the Central African Republic placed first.
- The Ecological Footprint Index, which ranks Canada 135th among 138 countries and the U.S. 138th—making Canada and the U.S. two of the four worst countries in the world environmentally.
- The University of Victoria's "Canada vs. the OECD" index, which ranks Canada twenty-eighth out of the twenty-nine developed democracies (and the U.S., in last place, twenty-ninth).

Ms. Petersen and Mr. Samson examined these rankings, observing first the obvious: "In some of these reports, Canada appears to be among the best environmental stewards. In others, Canada is one of the least successful." They found that all of the rankings exhibited "an underlying ideology," and many of them were "counter-intuitive." They concluded succinctly: "These reports have limited value." They warned that governments should not base public policy on any of them.

It is the last of these six rankings that has emerged as environmental dogma in Canada. Canadians are not guilt-ridden enough to believe that we rank 135th out of 138—but they do apparently find it credible to think that we might rank at the bottom of the wealthy, developed nations. This set of rankings, at any rate, is the most-quoted in Canada—and almost always in a misleading way. Thus, in a speech to the Ottawa Economics Association last year, NDP Leader Jack Layton quoted the dismal "Canada vs. the OECD" findings in a way that appeared to attribute them to the Organization for Economic Cooperation and Development itself. (Introducing error into a dubious finding, expressing it as a simple matter of fact, he said: "Canada ranks twenty-seven out of twenty-eight OECD countries on the environment.") The Paris-based OECD, a principal research agency of the world's developed democracies, of course publishes environmental data—but has never produced a country-by-country ranking and, indeed, offers no interpretation of its data. As Environment Canada's forensic analysis of these reports demonstrated, these environmental rankings aren't worth the paper they are printed on.

If national wealth determines environmental investment, as it does, how can the richest country in the world rank environmentally as one of the world's worst countries? (In the Yale–Columbia ESI, the United States got ranked sixty-third, alongside Bhutan and Cuba.) The explanation is this: all of the environmental rankings are based on an inherent bias toward small countries. Yale–Columbia's Top Three in its EPI rankings are New Zealand, Sweden, and Finland; the Top Three in its ESI rankings are Finland, Norway, and Uruguay. Indeed, in the

ESI rankings, the runners-up are Sweden, Iceland, and Canada. In a candid admission, Yale–Columbia concedes that its methodology favours small countries with substantial natural resources and small populations.

Yale–Columbia's ESI, nevertheless, shows that the United States leads the world in a number of important categories, among them wilderness protection, capital investment, and technological innovation. It says, for example, that the U.S. has extended federal protection to 29.6 per cent of its forests; Canada to 8.9 per cent. The World Economic Forum Innovation Index, which measures the capacity of countries to produce technological innovation, ranks the United States as No. 1 (with a score of 6.44 out of 10; Canada, 4.45). UNESCO, by the way, says that the U.S. supports 4,099 researchers per million people; Canada 2,978.

The World Economic Forum Innovation Index also ranks countries by the international funding they provide for environmental projects. Calculated by population and expressed on a scale of 1 to 100, the index gives the United States a score of 40, Canada a score of 28.9. Furthermore, in a ranking of private-sector "sustainability," as measured by the Dow Jones Sustainability Index, U.S. big-cap companies make a more significant contribution to the environment than do comparable Canadian companies.

Like the Yale–Columbia reports, the World Economic Forum Innovation Index finds that the United States operates at a higher level of energy efficiency than Canada—with Canada in this assessment using 13.39 terajoules of energy per million dollars of GDP, and the U.S. using 8.89. (By contrast, the United Kingdom uses 5.86; Russia, 21.39.) Yet Canada's carbon emissions (per million dollars of GDP) are comparable: 168 metric tons per Canadian, 170 metric tons per American.

None of these U.S.-friendly findings appears to have influenced the most important of the Canadian rankings, the 2001 "Canada vs. the OECD: An Environmental Comparison." Written by University of Victoria environmental lawyer David Boyd, this was the report that ranked Canada number twenty-eight out of the twenty-nine countries that held membership in the OECD.

Though subsequently revised, *Canada vs. the OECD* retains many of its original dubious conclusions. It's this report that the David Suzuki Foundation cites to back up its assertion that Canada has one of the worst environmental records in the developed world—predictably exceeded only by the United States. In its original formulation, Mr. Boyd advanced his "dismal" finding unequivocally and as a strictly factual finding. "These results prove," he said, "that Canada has one of the poorest environmental records in the industrialized world."

They prove nothing of the kind. From a strictly common-sense perspective, ranking Canada and the United States as the world's environmentally worst countries is as absurd as ranking Mexico and Turkey as two of the world's environmentally best countries. Here are Mr. Boyd's final scores for the countries he placed top and bottom (lowest number of points wins): No. 1, Switzerland, score: 9.2; No. 2, Mexico, score: 10.2; No. 3, Turkey, score: 10.7; No. 28, Canada, score: 21.8; No. 29, U.S., score: 22.8.

In contrast, the Yale–Columbia Environmental Sustainability Index ranked Mexico seventy-third.

Fraser Institute researcher Heather Holden and professional engineer Jerry Sklenar took a close look at *Canada vs. the OECD* a couple of years ago and found it so deeply flawed as to be meaningless. Here are a few of their observations:

- Mr. Boyd ranked Canada twenty-seventh (out of twenty-eight) in forestry, based on our annual per capita harvest of trees—whereas he ranked Iceland, which has virtually no trees, first. If the rankings had been based on harvest per hectare of forest, Canada would have ranked sixth instead of twenty-seventh.
- Mr. Boyd ranked Canada twenty-fifth (out of twenty-eight) in fertilizer use, based on its annual per capita consumption—whereas he ranked Switzerland, which has 1 per cent of Canada's cropland, first. If this ranking had been based on fertilizer use per hectare of cropland, Canada would have ranked third, Switzerland eighteenth.
- Mr. Boyd ranked Canada twentieth (out of twenty-eight) on per capita catch in fisheries, which measure ignored the relative size of fishing grounds. He gave the best rankings to four land-locked countries with no marine and negligible freshwater fisheries: Austria, Switzerland, the Czech Republic, and Hungary.
- Mr. Boyd ranked Canada ranked twenty-seventh (out of twenty-eight) in energy consumption per capita, and awarded the top three rankings to the

least-developed OECD countries—Turkey, Mexico, and Portugal.

As Environment Canada's assessment found, ideology plays a decisive role in these ranking exercises. The distortions arise from a wide range of dubious assumptions—that poor societies are less destructive of the environment than rich societies, that socialist economies are less destructive than market economies, that countries with seven-digit populations are less destructive than countries with eight-digit or nine-digit populations. It goes without saying that left-liberal governments are less destructive than conservative governments.

On this last assumption, though, environmentalists are divided. Many Canadian environmentalists regard former Conservative prime minister Brian Mulroney as the greenest prime minister in Canadian history—as he was formally described last year at a bipartisan tribute to his environmental record. It was Mr. Mulroney who presided over the successful negotiation of a Canada–U.S. treaty on acid rain, who introduced an Environmental Protection Act, and who created eight new national parks. Many of these environmentalists regard Canada's last two Liberal prime ministers as national embarrassments. (For his part, Mr. Boyd, the author of the *Canada vs. the* OECD report, once dismissed former Liberal prime minister Jean Chrétien as "Canada's first antienvironmental prime minister, on a par with such U.S. presidents as Ronald Reagan and George Bush.")

But then the U.S. presidents with the best environmental records have generally been conservatives. It was President

Ulysses S. Grant, a "Radical Republican," who invented the national park. (Yellowstone, the first in the world, was created in 1872 by legislation designating it "as a pleasure ground for the enjoyment of the people.") It was Republican president Theodore Roosevelt (1901–1909), one of the faces on Mount Rushmore, who set aside 230 million acres of land for federal protection—five national parks, 150 national forests, fifty bird preserves, four game preserves. During his two terms as president, Roosevelt protected—on average, every day—another 84,000 acres of land.

Environmental protection is not, in fact, an ideological phenomenon. In a 2006 report, U.S. National Academy of Sciences researchers concluded that national income, not ideology, correlates directly with environmental protection. The report cited what it calls "forest transition" as a good example, defining the phenomenon as the point at which countries stop deforestation and begin to rebuild their forests. "No nation where annual per capita gross domestic product exceeds $4,600," the report concludes, "has had a negative rate [of change in forest growth]." In other words, richer countries replace their forests and expand them. Poorer countries consume them.

The United States now adds forest lands every year—and has done so for many years. Indeed, the U.S. reached its "forest transition" in the late 1800s. "In Connecticut, where the first U.S. forest transition occurred, forests expanded from 30 per cent of the state in 1860 to 60 per cent in 2002."

This is not only an American phenomenon. In El Salvador (per capita GDP: $5,600), the amount of land with 25 per cent tree cover (or more) expanded from 72 per cent to 93 per cent between 1992 and 2001. Other countries with expanding forests include the Dominican Republic (per capita GDP: $6,700) and China (per capita GDP: $7,700). By planting 4 million hectares of forest a year, China has reversed Asia's deforestation all by itself. In the decade from 1990 to 1999, Asia lost 792,000 hectares of forest a year. In the last five years, it has added one million hectares a year.

The U.N.'s Food and Agricultural Organization (FAO), meantime, reports that the global rate of deforestation is slowing, that deforestation is now exclusively a phenomenon of poverty. The poorest countries of Africa account for half of the deforestation; the poorest regions of South America account for the rest.

The wealthiest countries are all expanding forests at a rapid rate—Europe by a million hectares a year. The world has increased protected forests and conservation land by more than 30 per cent since 1990—which means that 400 million hectares of the earth's surface have been designated as protected, or 10 per cent of the forests of earth. In the United States, President George W. Bush has followed the example of Teddy Roosevelt a century ago. During his presidency, so far, the U.S. has added 10 million hectares of conservation land—38,000 square miles. In the last five years—the George W. Bush years—the U.S. has added 146 million metric tons of biomass a year to its forests. This increase in biomass provides a trap that can hold 9 per cent of net U.S. carbon emissions a year.

The United States has made great gains in cleansing its air—ever since Republican president Richard Nixon established the Environmental Protection Agency in 1970 as an independent guardian of the nation's environment and put a crusader named William D. Ruckelshaus in charge of it. The EPA has remained famously, not to say notoriously, independent. Unlike the environmental agencies in some other countries, such as Canada, the EPA does not need to consult with the agriculture department before taking action.

The Clean Air Act, another Richard Nixon initiative, authorized the EPA to act alone, on its own counsel—a power often contested in court by corporations. In a signal decision in 2001, the U.S. Supreme Court unanimously ruled—in a judgment written by a conservative justice, Antonin Scalia— that the EPA did not need to concern itself with the cost of the regulations it imposes to ensure that air quality remains high.

"The Clean Air Act unambiguously bars cost considerations from federal air quality regulations," Mr. Justice Scalia wrote in this judgment. "The EPA is required to set air quality standards at the level that is requisite—that is, neither lower or higher than is necessary—to protect the public health with an adequate margin of safety."

In Los Angeles, of course, air quality problems remain— especially in Hollywood. The UCLA Institute of the Environment has found that the film industry emits 140,000 tons a year of ozone precursors and particulates, the highest emitter of these pollutants except for coastal oil refineries. Further, the institute identified the film industry as the number three source of GHG emissions in L.A.—in part because the trailers provided to movie stars are frequently powered by dirty diesel generators. Under the circumstances, this must be regarded as an inconvenient truth.

All wealthy countries have made great gains in air quality, of course—though the former Soviet Bloc countries drag down the European averages, as they do with GHG emissions. Put the rich European countries together and you can show that Europe produces less GHG emissions than the United States. Put all of Europe's GHG emissions together (excluding the Soviet Bloc countries, which reduced emissions only by shutting down dirty, derelict factories), and you can show that Americans are now doing better on GHG emissions than Europeans.

From 1990 through 2004, as noted, the United States increased GHG emissions by 12 per cent, Canada by 24 per cent; yet Spain increased its emissions by 44.7 per cent in the same period. Portugal by 36.7 per cent. Ireland by 25.6 per cent. Greece by 25.8 per cent. Finland by 21.5 per cent. and Austria by 16.5 per cent.

The simple fact is that Kyoto wasn't needed to use energy more efficiently. Consider, for comparison purposes, the unilateral reduction in hydrocarbon emissions from cars and trucks in the United States in the past forty years. In the 1960s, these emissions averaged 10.2 grams per mile. In the 1970s, they averaged 1.8 grams per mile. In the 1980s, they averaged 0.4 grams per mile. As reported by the EPA in 2004, they now average 0.2 grams per mile. Hydrocarbon emissions, a source of particulates found in air pollution, have fallen by 99.3 per cent in forty years.

As you would reasonably expect from the wealthiest nation, the United States is simply a greener place than much of continental Europe. The U.S. now has the lowest levels of air pollution it has ever recorded. California's wineries put more VOCs (volatile organic compounds) into the atmosphere than California's cars. U.S. stocks of ocean fish are on the rise. U.S. forests are expanding at ten times the rate of Europe's forests. U.S. wetlands are increasing by 25,000 acres a year. Forty years ago, the American bald eagle had a close call with extinction. Now there are 7,500 breeding pairs.

Carbon monoxide emissions have fallen by 70.6 per cent since 1970. Nitrogen-oxide emissions have fallen by 45.8 per cent. Sulphur-dioxide emissions have fallen by 58.0 per cent. VOC emissions have fallen by 67 per cent. These trends will continue, with Kyoto or without Kyoto. (The EPA anticipates that emissions from cars and trucks will decline by another 80 per cent in the next twenty-five years.)

Cleaner air? In Los Angeles? The EPA's Air Quality Index measures pollution on a scale that runs from 1 to 500. A reading higher than 100 signals a "threshold level" of unhealthy air. In the 1980s, Los Angeles experienced 1,762 health-alert days. In the 1990s, it experienced 658 health-alert days—a decline of 62.7 per cent. Every metropolitan American city experienced comparable improvements—San Diego by 69.4 per cent, Philadelphia by 43.9 per cent, Cincinnati by 58.5 per cent, New York by 50.9 per cent.

Dioxins? Between 1982 and 2002, the U.S. eliminated 92 per cent of environmental dioxins. The EPA now says that the biggest source of dioxins are backyard trash fires. Lead from gasoline? Once common in babies' blood, it's now gone. Toxins in the environment? The EPA's Toxic Release Inventory (TRI) reports that industrial toxins have fallen by 60 per cent since 1988, its baseline year. This decrease means that 2 billion tons of toxic material a year are not getting dumped into the environment.

suvs? According to the Pacific Research Institute and the American Enterprise Institute, suvs have produced the same voc emissions as regular cars since the 1996 model year. They have produced the same nitrogen-oxide emissions as regular cars since the 2001 model year. Average vehicle emissions—for cars and for suvs—are falling by 10 per cent a year.

In some ways, Europeans do indeed pace the world in environmental protection. These achievements, however, are not continental. They are local, regional, national—precisely as achievements are in the United States and in Canada. This is why it will be futile to seek environmental solutions by inducing slower rates of economic growth. The world is green to the degree that it is rich—and greenest precisely in the places where it is richest. By and large, the world has all the global conscience it can afford.

OUR MYTHOLOGY
OF VALUES

BY ANDREW COHEN

IN THE SUMMER OF 2007, Nicolas Sarkozy, the newly elected president of France, made his first big executive decision: he would
spend his holidays in America. He would go to the lakes of
New Hampshire and the salons of Boston. Not to the Riviera,
not to the Alps, not to the Loire Valley, where *le président* was
supposed to go. America! When he was asked why, upon his
return, Sarkozy offered a sweet hymn to the Hyperpower.

"I adored New England," he told the *New York Times*.

> I loved Boston. I thought it was an extraordinarily
> beautiful city, with a remarkable quality of life. I love
> the kindness and the simplicity of the people.... I loved
> the way the people made us feel welcome. I liked the
> countryside. I like the malls where people go shopping.
> I like the restaurants. I like swimming in the lakes. I like
> going jogging in the woods.... I like the way people are
> relaxed and uncomplicated. And I don't know why I
> should have given up going to the United States
> because a small part of the French elite professes an
> anti-Americanism that in no way corresponds to what
> the French people think—in no way at all.

The decision was unpopular in some quarters, but the self-confident Sarkozy was unfazed. He recalled that France and America were old allies, going back to their origins in the late eighteenth century, and they had never been at war with each other. There was no need to see each other as enemies now, he said, as detractors like to paint the two peoples. We have always helped each other, he said, remembering the Americans in the Second World War and the role played by Lafayette and Rochambeau in the American Revolution. More important, he argued, the United States and France share universal values. "I think [they] are much more alike than they think," he said. "Much more. It is rare to find two countries in the world that think their ideas are universal." The Germans, the Russians, the Chinese, the Italians, and the Spanish don't see themselves that way. "We think [our] ideas are destined to illuminate the world," he said. "And perhaps that is the source of competition between us. It's perhaps the fact that we are alike."

This was an extraordinary statement from a president of France, a hotbed of anti-Americanism in recent years. It was extraordinary not only because Sarkozy found nice things to say about those tasteless, unsophisticated Americans, contradicting the stereotype presented by commentators such as Bernard-Henri Lévy in *American Vertigo*, an amusing catalogue of Old World prejudices. It was even more extraordinary because Sarkozy was prepared to say that the two peoples are actually *alike* in their thinking. Alike. Quel horreur! The French and the Americans, he declares unapologetically, are similar because they share universal values. And he's not afraid to say it.

For a Canadian, what is striking about these sentiments is that they would be unthinkable coming from a prime minister of Canada, at least none who has held office in the last decade and a half. To speak with honest, unabashed affection of the United States, to speak kindly, without artifice, of the American people and their way of life, to suggest that we share the same fundamental values—this is not the way of a Canadian leader. It is not the way of our leaders, because it would challenge our deep, abiding, and necessary orthodoxy that the Americans are not like us and we are not like them.

Fundamentally, this is the greatest of our mythologies about the United States. Oh, our leaders like to crow about the world's longest undefended border and the world's largest trading relationship, even if terrorism is threatening one and China is eroding the other. And they like to recall John F. Kennedy, who told us that geography has made us neighbours and history has made us friends, which is no less true now than it was in 1961.

At root, though, few of us think ourselves alike. Certainly not our politicians, who don't think it's in their interest to be seen as too close to the Americans (which is how Jean Chrétien could criticize Brian Mulroney for having gone fishing with George H. Bush, while he played golf with Bill Clinton, surreptitiously). Even Stephen Harper, who was pro-American while in Opposition, felt a need in 2007 to tell the Australian parliament, in referring to the Americans, that "we are fiercely proud of our differences." We note these differences even though there are probably no two peoples on earth today more alike in their values than Canadians and

Americans. So, questions demand answers. What is the nature of this difference of values that we assert, the greatest of our American myths? How does it manifest itself in our politics? And why does it endure in our successful country?

———

In 2003, Michael Adams, one of Canada's leading pollsters, published *Fire and Ice: The United States, Canada and the Myth of Converging Values*. His argument is that the two countries are not becoming more alike; actually, in their fundamental values, they are drifting apart. He bases his thesis on three large opinion surveys he took on both sides of the border in 1992, 1996, and 2000. His book challenges the prevailing notion of cultural and economic integration expressed by many on the millennium, especially historian Michael Bliss and journalist Jeffrey Simpson, who argued that "Canadians, whether they like it or not, have never been more like Americans, and Canadian society has never been more similar to that of the United States." Balderdash, says Adams. Brandishing charts and figures, he argues that it isn't so at all. Americans, in their tastes, habits of mind, and political and economic choices, are a fundamentally different people.

How? Well, for starters, they are materialistic, violent, vulgar, and superficial. Canadians are less so. If minivans outsell suvs in Canada by two to one, says Adams, this is "a stark difference which can be traced directly to the differing values of our two countries." His conclusion: we care more about the environment than they do. He draws many other conclusions, too, claiming that Canadians are, in general, more liberal, more autonomous, more tolerant of diversity.

Most telling was the Canadian response to the book, which came out two months after Canada refused to join the United States in Iraq and a week after a simmering George W. Bush cancelled his visit to Ottawa. The book became a bestseller and drew favourable reviews. Its thesis was unquestioned. Paul Martin, the prime minister, called it "a very accurate portrayal of social conditions." It won a prestigious literary prize as a book on public policy, and was named one of the hundred most important Canadian books by the *Literary Review of Canada*. Later on, when critics re-examined Adams's numbers, considered the political and social trends, and declared his thesis thin, the early reception to *Fire and Ice* raised an important question: why were we so enthusiastic? In the answer, we realized something equally important: this wasn't about Adams. It was about us.

What Adams was providing, at a time when the direction and the leadership of the United States were losing favour in Canada, was a rationale for a primordial instinct in our character. Among Canadians, there is a distrust, a suspicion, a feeling of insecurity toward the Americans. It is an instinct that seeks to create differences between us and them, even when there are actually very few. It is, to use Freud's phrase, the narcissism of small differences. Put plainly, we have a need to differentiate when there isn't that much to differentiate, arising from a lack of self-confidence that comes from sharing a continent with a neighbour about nine times our size in population. Canadians may not know what we are—the search for self-definition and identity has eluded us—but we know who we aren't. And, by God, we aren't those damn Americans!

So, we have created a comforting mythology about the United States and us, and no more so than when it comes to fundamental values. This is captured nicely in the theory of divergence—that alleged yawning gap between Canadians and Americans—which was proffered so persuasively by Michael Adams in *Fire and Ice* and fell on such receptive ears in Canada. But what was it about this meditation on the Canadian psyche that seemed to resound so deeply? Why did smart people seem to abandon their critical faculties and fall in love with divergence, in the face of evidence to the contrary? The answer may be simply that Adams was telling us what we wanted to hear.

It works this way: we have long had a feeling of moral superiority toward the United States, rooted in a feeling that we are a kinder, gentler people. This has been around since our beginnings in 1867. "We are free from many of the social cancers that are empoisoning the national life of our neighbours," declared the *Canadian Methodist Magazine* in the 1880s. "We have no polygamous Mormondon; no Ku-Klux terrorism; no Oneida Communists; no Illinois divorce system; no cruel Indian massacres." Not all of this was true—the arriving Europeans had rendered the Beothuk of Newfoundland extinct by the early nineteenth century—but there is no doubt that we did not have the same history of violence and we thought differently of government. This gave Canada a certain hauteur. As historian J.L. Granatstein put it in a speech: "Canada may have been poorer, but it was better, an attitude that remained all the way into the twentieth century and into the twenty-first." Dean Acheson, the rigid, patrician secretary of state under Harry Truman, saw this in our diplomacy in the 1940s and 1950s. He resented Canada's lecturing the United States during the Korean War, fuming in a memo at "you moralizing, interfering Canadians." In 1966, long out of power but not out of breath, he wrote an acerbic chapter for a collection of essays on Canadian-American relations. He called it, pointedly, "Canada: Stern Daughter of the Voice of God."

This smugness—a superiority of values—has burrowed deep into our political culture. It erupts from time to time, usually in sulphurous ways. The most recent example was in the election campaign of 2005–2006, when Paul Martin's Liberals were trailing Stephen Harper's Conservatives. Martin went to Montreal to attend a conference on the Kyoto Accord, where he accused the United States of lacking "a global conscience." The inconvenient truth was that Canada had a poorer record under Kyoto than its neighbour, relatively speaking; while emissions in the United States had risen 13 per cent since 1990, Canada's had soared 24 per cent. But that didn't stop Martin, who knew that bashing the Americans plays well among Canadians. If that meant trafficking in hyperbole and hypocrisy, so be it.

When David Wilkins, the United States ambassador in Ottawa, heard Martin's reprimand, he said: "It may be smart election-year politics to thump your chest and constantly criticize your friends and your number-one trading partner. But it's a slippery slope." Later, he added: "Canada never has to tear down the United States to build itself up." Actually, we do.

You do this when you feel inferior. Poor Wilkins, who had been in Ottawa only seven months, didn't get Canada. He knew that it is smart politics to attack the United States, which is why Martin's numbers rose the next day. What he didn't know is that making moral distinctions is terribly important to Canadians. It makes us feel better about ourselves. We need to create differences between us and them. That the differences may be narrow, that they may be overstated, that they may not even exist does not matter; inventing and nourishing those differences sustains an irrepressible and indispensable Canadian nationalism. This is the purest form of narcissism, and we see it conspicuously in our view of Americans.

Hence, the regime of differences we have created about the United States. There are many, and each, in its way, seeks to flatter us. Consider, for example, that hoary belief that Canada is a mosaic and America a melting pot. This is stamped early upon young Canadians, as if it were religious doctrine. Like other Canadian mythologies, it bristles with self-righteousness. The sentiment here is that Canada welcomes immigrants and allows them—nay, encourages them—to retain their languages and customs. *We* let them be who they are. *We* do not ask them to assimilate.

The mosaic may be true of Canada, but is the United States the melting pot we imagine? Hardly. The rise of Hispanic America, which swelled by 58 per cent in the 1990s, has made Latinos a strong visible minority—if not a majority— in Florida, California, Texas, Arizona, New Mexico, and Nevada. Pockets can be found in New York, New Jersey, and Washington, D.C., where automatic banking machines offer instructions in Spanish as they do French in Canada. Of course, there's a reason: the U.S. Census Bureau reported in 2004 that 31 million of the 41 million Hispanic Americans (there are thought to be millions more now) spoke Spanish at home. That is not a melting pot as we imagine it. The diversity of America is reflected in its politics, too. When the 2008 presidential race began, a black-American and a Hispanic-American were running for the Democrats. A Mormon and an Italian-American were running for the Republicans. Any one of them might be elected president. It challenges the notion, as Michael Adams puts it, that Canadians, who love to trumpet their multiculturalism, "are more tolerant of diversity than Americans." It is reason to reconsider, as we cling to the self-satisfying idea that we have got immigration right and the Americans have got it wrong.

Immigration is one of the misconceptions about the United States that take root in Canada and flower in our well-watered imagination. There are many others—on rates of savings, levels of obesity, and political values—that encourage Canadians to feel superior about themselves and their values. On closer inspection, though, are we really so different, after all?

We have long believed, for example, that we are savers and the Americans are spenders. Like every other distinction, there is an implied value here. Savers are prudent, measured, virtuous. That would be us. Spenders are reckless, wanton, profligate. That would be them. While this may have once been true—Canadians used to save more than Americans up to a few years ago—it no longer is. As Canadians have become wealthier, they have developed an instinct to spend. When our dollar reached parity with and surpassed the American dollar in 2007, bargain-hungry shoppers descended on border towns in New York, overwhelming customs facilities. According to statistics, the savings rate in Canada has now fallen into negative territory, below that of the United States. Whatever the reason, the fact is that Canadians are saving less money, about as little as the Americans. Frugality is no longer a point of distinction between us and them.

Neither is physical fitness. Once we were fit and they were fat. Like everywhere else, the Obese American is a caricature in Canada; we sneer at the corpulent American who can barely squeeze into the airplane seat beside us. Obesity is an epidemic below the forty-ninth parallel, where half the population is considered overweight. In Canada, too, we are no longer on the side of the svelte. Since the 1980s, Canadians have also been getting heavier. Today, about a third of Canadians are overweight. More alarming, the rate of growth in obesity is about the same on both sides of the border. As the *Ottawa Citizen* editorialized in 2006: "It is getting harder and harder to be self-righteous and denigrate the Americans for their super-sized lifestyle—a lifestyle we evidently share."

Most profoundly, the convergence of values characterizes our politics. The perception among Canadians is that we are white knights and they are black knights. We see "American-style politics" as inherently undemocratic—rough, corrupt, shallow. The influence of money, the length of campaigns, the apathy of voters, the distemper of the debate, the disenfranchisement of blacks and the poor are among those elements that colour our unsavoury image. Of course, much of this is true; money does dominate the process in the United States. Campaigns are interminable, and broken voting machines and "Swiftboat" tactics are reprehensible. But the idea that our politics is more open, responsive, and progressive—let alone *democratic*—isn't necessarily true anymore, if it ever was.

Democratic? Not so. The concentration of power in the Office of the Prime Minister was so total during Jean Chrétien's decade in power, with successive majorities, that author Jeffrey Simpson called it "the friendly dictatorship." Unlike the United States, we have few referenda and no means of petition, review, or recall. Our party leaders are picked by delegates chosen by riding associations in meetings often tainted by allegations of corruption. Our leaders are not made to prove themselves by running a gauntlet of state primaries and caucuses covering half the country. We have no history of public hearings on prime-ministerial appointments, judicial, bureaucratic, or diplomatic. While a broader range of views can be represented in a multi-party parliament, our two governing parties are largely centrist, with fewer differences between them than the Republicans and Democrats. Voter turnout is only marginally higher in Canada. As for civility in our political discourse, we abandoned that conceit some time ago. The debate in the House of Commons is often abusive and personal; in 2006 a minister crudely alluded to a female member of the Opposition, his former girlfriend, as "a dog." Our televised leadership debates often descend into shouting and name-calling. And the parties, especially the Conservatives, are now running "attack ads"—as they did against Liberal leader Stéphane Dion in early 2007—as vicious as those used by the Americans, and, very possibly, inspired by them. No wonder former prime ministers dislike each other so intensely, as we saw in the publication of the score-settling memoirs of Brian Mulroney and Jean Chrétien in the autumn of 2007. The office simply doesn't impose upon its former occupants the same kind of discipline and dignity as the presidency, which is no less hotly contested.

In many ways, the values of our political culture are becoming increasingly American. We have begun to ask high-court judicial appointees to testify before a parliamentary committee. We have fixed the dates of federal elections, and some in the provinces, too. We have passed a law appointing a special prosecutor, like the Americans. We are debating the idea of appointing senators from those elected, as well as limiting their terms of office. We have created a national military cemetery in Ottawa, in the words of the former chief of the defence staff, "like the one in Arlington, Virginia." The leaders of the two big political parties no longer have two or three chances to run for office; like presidential candidates, if they lose the first time, they may not get a second. All this is American in tone. And the most Americanizing element of our lives in the last quarter-century? Why, the Charter of Rights and Freedoms.

At the same time, the language of our politics is changing. We speak of "administration" rather than government, and "Mr. Prime Minister" rather than Prime Minister, and "inside the Queensway," much like Washington's Beltway. We sometimes address former ambassadors by that title, as if they keep the honorific, which they don't in Canada. Stephen Harper is fond of saying, "God Bless Canada."

As we are becoming more American in our politics, it is also fair to say that they are becoming more like us. In the 2008 presidential primaries, the top domestic issue was health care. Every major candidate had a plan. The chances are good that the United States will adopt a form of universal health care, though not as extensive as ours or the Europeans, before this decade is out. When it does, it will eliminate one of those deep-seated differences between us and them. It will be harder to say they are less compassionate. There are signs the next president will adopt a more engaged, multilateral foreign policy, which will also cheer Canadians, who believe in international institutions. It is also likely that the next president will come not from the sunbelt but from New York, Massachusetts, or Illinois, parts of the United States that know us better. While it is too soon to declare "a liberal hour" in the United States, there are demographic signs it is on its way. If so, it will show, once again, a narrowing of differences in values. Already, as someone once quipped, there are more Americans in California who think like Canadians than there are Canadians in Canada.

What all this reflects is what Nicolas Sarkozy could say about America but Stephen Harper could not—even if he believes it—because Canadians do not want to hear it. And that is that our values, in their fundamentals, are much the same. This isn't to say that our political culture is not at all different, as Quebec is different from Texas. Of course it is, in many ways; thankfully, the influence of religion in politics and the stature of guns in America have no parallel in Canada. Yet on the big questions—democracy, freedom, human rights, the free market, pluralism, diversity—we are largely at one. It is important to remind ourselves that it was a Canadian, John Humphrey, who drafted the Universal Declaration of Human Rights, and an American, Eleanor Roosevelt, who chaired the committee that presented it to the United Nations. One day, when we are more self-confident people, we will understand that these are the values that matter and these are the beliefs we share, whatever the useful mythology we have created.

CAN CANADA BE AS INNOVATIVE, COMPETITIVE, AND ENTREPRENEURIAL AS THE UNITED STATES?

JESSICA LECROY

WHICH OF OUR TWO COUNTRIES—Canada or the United States—is best positioning itself to take advantage of the new globalized, knowledge-based economy in the long run, for 2050? The answer may not be as obvious as public perceptions in both countries suggest. The debate, however, is both critical and healthy as we each respond to challenges posed by "the new economy" and come to grips with our respective national concepts of public goods and entitlements.

Canadians may in fact be correct in thinking that, in general, Americans believe their northern neighbour pays too high a price in terms of competitiveness for an idyllic claim of being "kinder and gentler" than the United States. The myth-buster is that Canadians themselves are beginning to think this as well. An alarm has been sounded that the quality and way of life that Canadians value—and proudly use to distinguish their country from the U.S.—could be squandered before mid-century by nothing more than a simple lack of initiative. Such a development would not be good for Canada, or for America. Ironically, this Canadian re-evaluation comes at a time when the United States, stoked by the 2008 presidential campaign, is examining the same issues through an American prism that is not reflecting, at the moment, a particularly confident light.

In 2008 and 2009, we are likely to see far more comparisons between Canada and the U.S. across a range of issues, heretofore mostly focused on health care, that will indicate how well each of the two countries prepares our populations to prosper in this new economy. One of these areas that needs much more in-depth comparative analysis is the public commitment to providing our workforces with the education and skills they must have to be innovative, competitive, and entrepreneurial in a global economy.

"Skate to Where the Puck Is Going To Be"

As with most things in life, hockey provides insight: "Skate to where the puck is going to be, not to where it is or has been," the Great One, Wayne Gretzky (or his father Walter), advised.

The Toronto Maple Leafs may provide an encouraging object lesson: the Leafs have not won a Stanley Cup in forty years. Their record is chronically mediocre—they have won 1,298 regular-season games and lost 1,378 in the same period, with a 12–12 win-loss record more than a quarter of the way through the 2007–08 season. They sign second-rate talent to long-term contracts and trade good draft picks for meagre returns. The team hasn't even made the playoffs in the last two years.

CAN CANADA BE AS INNOVATIVE, COMPETITIVE, AND ENTREPRENEURIAL AS THE UNITED STATES?

Index Rankings: Canada and the U.S.

Index Title	Top 3 Countries	Canada's Rank	U.S. Rank
World Economic Forum's Global Competitiveness Index (2006-2007)	US, Switzerland, Denmark	13	1
2007 Economist Intelligence Unit Business Environment Rankings (Forecast 2008-2012)	Denmark, Finland, Singapore	4	9
World Bank's Doing Business Report 2008: Ease of Doing Business Ranking	Singapore, New Zealand, US	7	3
Index of Economic Freedom 2007: Heritage Foundation and the Wall Street Journal	Hong Kong, Singapore, Australia	10	4
Economic Freedom of the World Index 2007: The Fraser Institute Study (rankings are for 2005)	Hong Kong, Singapore, New Zealand	7	5
IMF GDP Per Capita for 2007: World Economic Outlook Database 2007	Luxembourg, Ireland, Norway	14	4
2007/2008 UN Human Development Index	Iceland, Norway, Australia	4	12
Transparency International Index: 2007 Corruption Perceptions Index ranks	Denmark, Finland, New Zealand	9	20
EIU Global Peace Index	Norway, New Zealand, Denmark	8	96
EIU Democracy Index 2006	Sweden, Iceland, Netherlands	9	17
The Anholt Nation Brands Index: Quarter 2 2007 results	UK, Germany, France	4	10
IMD's World Competitiveness Scoreboard 2007	USA, Singapore, Hong Kong	10	1
World Database of Happiness: Average Happiness in 95 Nations (1995-2005)	Denmark, Switzerland, Austria	9-14	17

"How can they be the most lucrative hockey team on the planet," playing to a sold-out crowd at every game, an article in *Forbes* magazine recently asked?[1]

Forbes calculated that the Leafs' parent company had in less than ten years tripled "the enterprise value" of the privately held parent company to US$1.5 billion.[2] Of this sum, the Leafs account for $413 million of value. The team's operating income for the 2006–07 season was set at over $52 million, an increase last season of 24 per cent. The next-most-valuable team, the New York Rangers, has an enterprise value of $365 million, and, at $25.4 million, less than half its rival's operating income.

The Maple Leafs' success is attributable to a range of enterprising factors: clever marketing, shrewd deal-making, savvy expansion, and diversification of the business. There is a new state-of-the-art arena (not funded by taxpayers!) that is used three hundred days a year, the acquisition of the Raptors basketball team and some TV channels, and a new soccer team, among other things that also included a salary cap. Now the strength of the loonie has added additional "oomph," since the team collects revenues in Canadian dollars and pays players' salaries in U.S. dollars. "Sports valuations," the magazine pointed out, "are founded on more than just championships; they are also a function of player costs, stadium real estate and the population of the home market."

Also what differentiates the Maple Leafs from other professional sports teams is its ownership. The team is not "a plaything of the rich or an excuse to fill airtime by a media conglomerate." The parent company is controlled by 270,000 schoolteachers via the private equity arm of one of Canada's largest and most profitable institutional investors, the Ontario Teachers' Pension Plan, which itself appears to have outmanoeuvred Wall Street to close the biggest leveraged buyout in history, $37 billion for the Canadian telecommunications company BCE.

The Leafs story sprang from a troubled history and a remarkable turnaround that recasts success as a process. It included managed risk, sound fundamentals, seized opportunities, some uncertainty, surprises, and trials and errors. All are elements associated with an entrepreneurial impulse building steady momentum towards full realization. What will it take to achieve excellence, a winning season, perhaps a championship? More importantly, however, will failure to make the playoffs for yet another year begin to erode the fan base and ticket sales, prompt the OTP to calculate the opportunity costs in lost playoff revenues, or increase demand for a new, more exciting (and winning), team in the region?

Canada is not the Leafs, but the Leafs provide a useful example of forward thinking and creative response for both the Canadian government (at the macroeconomic level) and Canadian businesses (at the microeconomic level). Like the Leafs, Canada's solid "valuation" will be increased—and it can rise to the top of the global league—by improving its performance on "ice" (innovation, competitiveness, and entrepreneurship).

Canada appears ready to proceed apace in a way that may, in the long run, prove equally instructive to the United States.

"I Was Told I Was Too Small, Too Slow, and I Would Never Make the NHL"

Where does Canada stand in terms of economic competitiveness? On the World Economic Forum's Global Competitive Index for 2007–08, Canada slipped to thirteenth place. This puts Canada behind a number of other sparsely populated Western economies that boast strong social programs. Highly ranked Switzerland, Denmark, Sweden, Finland, and the Netherlands do not enjoy Canada's bounty of natural resources or direct proximity to the world's biggest single-country consumer market. The Nordic countries have higher taxes than Canada, but they outrank Canada and the U.S. in a number of the 113 factors the Index evaluates, such as macroeconomic conditions (running budget surpluses, low levels of public indebtedness), efficient institutions, and higher education and training programs. These countries' economies, according to the report, are more open than Canada to innovation, competition, and high-impact entrepreneurship. They are the mature New Economy economies.

Today, at least, the United States is the global league's declared "champion" in terms of economic competitiveness. The World Economic Forum's Global Competitiveness Index and accompanying report has confirmed the U.S.'s top position for a second year running, citing the dynamism, innovation, efficiency, sophistication, and productivity of its entrepreneurial economy. These strengths are so considerable, the report held, that they may be sufficient to carry the current faltering economy through a cycle of huge deficits, financial weaknesses, lower consumer confidence and demand, as well as higher oil prices.[3]

CAN CANADA BE AS INNOVATIVE, COMPETITIVE, AND ENTREPRENEURIAL AS THE UNITED STATES?

This claim will undoubtedly be tested over the next year, as the U.S. edges towards outright recession in 2008. The world holds the United States responsible for the sub-prime mortgage excesses (estimated at $300 billion in the years to come) that have created spillover turbulence in the global credit markets. The American people are scrutinizing the half-trillion-dollar cost of the war in Iraq, equal to a $20,000 assessment against each American household. The new engine of global growth, the emerging economies, is expected to supplement some of the demand that will help mitigate a U.S. drag on the world economy.[4]

In the end, however, most everyone expects the United States will get out of the economic penalty box and back into play—a little humbled and more carefully monitored—because of its entrepreneurial resilience. The excesses that put it there are a costly aberration of what on the positive side makes it the world's most successful economy.[5]

Broadly held perceptions among Canadian and American economists and business people is that Canada is skating around the neutral zone of the rink while the United States charges the goal. Canadians themselves are now complaining that they "don't work hard or smart," that they are "adrift in underachievement," "mired in mediocrity" and "collective complacency," no longer even "going for the bronze." There is a sense among Canadians that they may have been de-incentivized by an overly generous social safety net that is propped up by inefficient government regulations, services, and programs, outdated union structures, high taxes, old machinery and equipment, and volatile commodity resources.[6]

Soaring demand for Canada's commodities have indeed put the country in a good economic space for now. Economic growth has been steady. Inflation is contained. Unemployment levels in 2007 have been at a thirty-three-year low. The Canadian dollar is strong. Government surpluses provide a strong fiscal base. Canada is the only one of the Group of 8 governments consistently operating in the black. The federal government posted a c$9.3 billion surplus for the first half of the 2007–08 fiscal year (not reflecting 4.8 billion in retroactive tax cuts that form part of a five-year c$60-billion tax-relief plan). Canada's population is culturally diverse, skilled, and educated. It has a good sectoral mix, in addition to its huge natural resources reserve. In some sectors, Canada outperforms the United States (see graph).[7]

Labour Productivity Levels In Canadian Industries, 2001

1. Primary metals	9. Transportation	17. Plastic and rubber products	25. Electrical equipment
2. Non-metallic mineral products	10. Motor vehicles	18. Utilities	26. Miscellaneous manufacturing
3. Wood products	11. Food, beverage and tobacco	19. Furniture and related products	27. Finance, insurance and real estate
4. Construction	12. Mining	20. Wholesale trade	28. Fabricated metal products
5. Other transportation equipment	13. Other services	21. Machinery	29. Computer and electronics
6. Printing and publishing	14. Business services	22. Textile and clothing	
7. Paper	15. Agriculture	23. Petroleum and coal products	
8. Chemicals	16. Retail trade	24. Information and cultural industries	

Industry by share of total business sector hours worked

Appears with permission of the Conference Board of Canada

158

CAN CANADA BE AS INNOVATIVE, COMPETITIVE, AND ENTREPRENEURIAL AS THE UNITED STATES?

Yet data suggests that, overall, Canada's productivity and standard of living, as compared with that of the United States, has declined, and will continue to decline over time—perhaps precipitously if a U.S. recession occurs or commodity prices dip.

Twenty years ago, a person's average income in Canada was just c$2,000 less than the average income in the United States. In 2005 the difference had increased to c$9,200. Canadians who work about the same hours as Americans nonetheless produce about 20 per cent less. Canada's status as a member of the G-7 is now being challenged. In 1990, Canada ranked fifth in the world in per capita income; now it is tenth. In attracting inward foreign direct investment relative to GDP, Canada ranks near the bottom of the thirty industrialized member countries of the OECD (the Organization for Economic Cooperation and Development), has the second-highest level of statutory restrictions on foreign ownership, and one of the highest marginal taxes on capital investment. The service sector constitutes over 60 per cent of Canada's domestic economy, yet service exports represent just over 12 per cent, well below the OECD average.

Canadian economists have done an excellent job in raising public awareness of these problems and the proposed solutions. What they may not have realized is how useful the Canadian insights are for an American audience, how much we in the United States can learn about ourselves when you gauge yourselves against us.

The Conference Board of Canada recently completed The Canada Project initiative, a three-year program of research and follow-on engagement with decision-makers and the public, to highlight Canada's lagging productivity performance. It provides a comprehensive roadmap, with specific recommendations to sustain Canada as one of the world's most successful economies: a) eliminating inter-provincial trade barriers in favour of a common market within Canada; b) encouraging innovation investment to accelerate growth; c) diversifying and expanding trade beyond the U.S., its dominant trading partner, and resource-based exports, to include the emerging economies and the service sectors; d) attracting more foreign investment; and e) addressing workforce shortage issues.

The Conference Board of Canada also issues annually "A Report Card on Canada," which benchmarks Canada's socio-economic performance against the United States and fifteen other top industrialized economies. Grades focus on outputs rather than inputs—on what has been achieved rather than on how much has been invested—to determine whether Canada is getting a good return on its investment and if new strategies should be considered. For example, in the innovation domain Canada gives itself a "D" and the U.S. a "B+"; on education, Canada gets an "A" and the U.S. gets a "C." Canada and the U.S. both receive a "D" on environmental issues.

Similarly, the Institute for Competitiveness and Prosperity is mandated to report directly to the public on Ontario's competitiveness, productivity, and capacity for innovation compared to other provinces and the United States. Its 2007 "Agenda for Canada's Prosperity" points out that, if Canada's "prosperity gap" with the U.S. is not narrowed, Canadians will be forced to accept a lower standard of living, with lower wages, fewer quality jobs, and less government revenue to support valued social programs and investments. This report attaches dollar values to the "gap" factors (e.g., underinvestment in capital equipment), which lowers Canada's productivity by C$500 per capita. If Canada's GDP were the same as the U.S.'s, the report calculates, the average Canadian household would have almost C$12,000 more in disposable income and the government C$108 billion in additional revenues.

Canada's Prosperity Gap

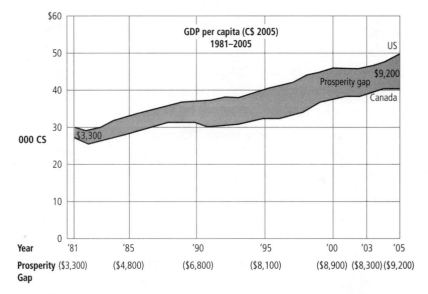

Year	'81	'85	'90	'95	'00	'03	'05
Prosperity Gap	($3,300)	($4,800)	($6,800)	($8,100)	($8,900)	($8,300)	($9,200)

Appears with permission of the Institute for Competitiveness and Prosperity

The Canada Institute at the Woodrow Wilson International Center's "One Issue, Two Voices" series also took up the productivity-gap issue to suggest that vibrant service-sector growth in the United States since 1995 is responsible for much of the productivity performance difference between our two countries.

"You Miss 100% of the Shots You Don't Take"

On September 28, 2007, Canadians held a parity party, cheering a moment of nationalistic pride—the loonie had achieved equality with the almighty greenback for the first time since 1967. The Canadian public checked the exchange rates with a level of intensity matched only by its interest in the proceedings of the Conrad Black trial. By November 7, with oil prices approaching US$100 a barrel, the loonie hit a modern-day record high of just over US$1.10. Accompanying any celebration and the lineup of eager cross-border Canadian shoppers flooding into the United States, however, was the sober recognition that the weakness in the U.S. economy and the rapid rise and volatility of the loonie would hurt Canada's U.S.-export-reliant economy, further imperil economic growth, and aggravate job losses.[8]

Canadians may have been right to celebrate the strong loonie, at least as a kind of harsh blessing in disguise. The loonie could be the sanest thing around if it levels out at or below parity. Responding to market forces, it sent the shrill signal needed to catalyze the restructuring Canada's economists have recommended for building a modern economy that is "ice-y" (innovative, competitive, and entrepreneurial). The strengthened loonie hands Canadian companies their impetus for change—their strongest incentive yet to take immediate action—to become more efficient and innovative, to diversify, expand, modernize, and brand themselves and their country as a global leader in the new economy. There was, in fact, a surprising admission by some Canadian businesses that a 20-per-cent currency exchange "subsidy" had discouraged smart business practices. With large commodity-based surpluses, a disciplined Canadian government has the temporary breathing room to enact and sponsor broad domestic reform that can be both pro-employment and pro-productivity.

Reforms suggested by Canadian economists are essential to enhance the benefits from globalization while addressing adjustment and inequality concerns. Canada has lost 300,000 manufacturing jobs since 2002. The U.S. has lost 5.5 million manufacturing jobs in the last decade, and China itself is now losing manufacturing jobs. Data indicates that technology improvements account for more manufacturing-job losses than globalization and outsourcing to cheaper production sites.

In real terms, the manufacturing sector does better by producing more high-value goods by fewer people as the path to prosperity. "High-road" manufacturing (high-skill, high-pay, high-performing), in which workers, unions, and management embrace productivity to secure jobs, is showing signs indicative of a rebound in both the United States and Canada. Cost differentials with the emerging economies are shrinking, companies are seeking the benefits of shorter supply chains, and consumers want quality goods that are made cleanly, intelligently, and efficiently. No one is seriously calling for the return of devalued "low-road" low-productivity, old-economy manufacturing jobs, whatever the pain level is now.[9]

"It's Essentially a Matter of Taking Care of What Takes Care of You"

Education is our most important weapon in fending off the downsides of the global economy. The next generation of policy choices that respond to the new economy challenges will be largely dependent upon productive workers.

While a multitude of factors affect a country's competitiveness, education is repeatedly singled out as a force multiplier for growth, productivity, and shared prosperity. If a country takes care of the education and skills training of its human capital, all other socio-economic factors of a country are improved—health care, the environment, the control of crime and corruption, as well as national economic performance. Educated workers are more engaged and make better life choices. They are better able to adapt to workplace change, to innovate and to create new products, services, and businesses. Studies indicate that a 1% increase in literacy and numeracy skills amounts to a 1.5% permanent increase in GDP; if the national average educational attainment level is increased by one year, aggregate productivity increases by 5%.[10]

In this regard, various studies indicate that Canada performs better (and at less cost) than the United States in preparing a larger relative number of its future generation of workers with the basic education and skills needed to become competent in a technologically complex and competitive environment.[11]

Canada's focus on high-quality, mainstream, publicly funded education for those between the ages of five and twenty-five places it at the top of the Group of 8, well ahead of the United States.[12] As a percentage of its GDP, Canada spends significantly less to support its educational institutions than the U.S. does: 5.93% versus 7.46% in the U.S. This equates to $6,482 per student at the secondary-school level, versus $9,590 per student in the United States.[13] The United States is not, by all accounts, getting as good a return on its investment as Canada. The late Senator Daniel Moynihan of New York once reportedly joked that the best way to improve general academic achievement in the U.S. would be to move all the states closer to Canada.

In the OECD's 2003 standardized assessment of fifteen-year-olds in math, reading, science, and problem-solving, Canadian students outscored American students in every category and ranking by a significant margin. Canada was singled out with Finland, Denmark, Iceland, Ireland, Norway, Poland, and Sweden for having high and consistent standards across schools and fewer socio-economic inequalities in learning opportunities. In Italy, Portugal, and the United States, over a quarter of the students were not proficient beyond Level 1 in mathematics, the lowest level on a six-level scale.[14]

Student access to and use of computers and the Internet is high in Canada compared to other OECD countries; eighty-nine per cent of fifteen-year-old Canadians have a home Internet connection, which ranks Canada second only to Sweden.[15] A separate U.S. Department of Education–sponsored comparative study of the reading-level attainment of ten-year-old fourth-graders from forty countries placed individually tested Canadian provinces in third, fifth, seventh, and sixteenth place, ahead of the U.S.'s position in eighteenth place, with only one Canadian province showing a slightly lower score.[16]

Both of our countries are grappling with "the silent epidemic" of secondary school dropout rates.[17] In an often-cited 2002 OECD study, Norway showed a dropout rate (defined as the share of twenty- to twenty-four-year-olds not in school and without a diploma or equivalent certificate) of only 4.6%, compared with Canada's 10.9% and the U.S.'s 12.3%. In the U.S., 2003 data indicated that approximately 3.5 million sixteen- to twenty-five-year-old Americans had dropped out of school; one out of three entering high school students will leave without a diploma and the odds are worse for minority students.[18]

In addition to having one of the world's highest rates of post-secondary education per capita, Canada also leads the world in its rate of college graduation. On the negative side, however, Canada produces a strikingly low proportion of advanced degrees, which means the U.S. performs better than Canada in the educational attainment of the older adult population, aged twenty-five to sixty-four. Canada also produces fewer university degrees in science and the technical disciplines needed to adapt to the demands of an innovating economy. Yet here too it is moving in a positive direction to address the problem.

In the recent annual global league table for excellence of the world's top two hundred universities, the London *Times* Higher Education Supplement and Qs ranking, noted that the U.S. and the U.K. had again in 2007 monopolized the champions listing of all the top ten universities, and dominated the top two hundred listing with fifty-seven universities from the U.S. and thirty-two from the U.K.[19]

Canada had eleven universities on the *Times* 200 list, all publicly funded. More revealing than the total number was that all but one had moved up significantly in the ranking. Particularly striking were those universities making the list for the first time, for example: Waterloo University at 112th place, up from 204th; the University of Western Ontario at 126th place, up from 215th; Simon Fraser at 139th, up from 282nd. Four Canadian universities made the *Times* list of top one hundred science universities—Toronto, McGill, British Columbia, and Waterloo—a surprisingly high number given Canada's existing public-funding goals to ensure broad access to university, as compared to the establishment of academically elite institutions that are often privately funded in the United States.

Canada compensates for the attainment gap in several ways. Historically, Canadian students have had the option of going outside the country for advanced degrees. Over 28,000 Canadians study in the U.S. alone, about half at the graduate level.[20] Frequently cited examples of the use of newly targeted private seed funding for excellence are the Perimeter Institute for Theoretical Physics and the Institute for Quantum Computing in Waterloo, Ontario. The University of Waterloo claims to employ more math teachers per student than any other university in the world. Canada's private sector is taking additional steps to lure back to Canada top scientists, researchers, and teachers, having taken note that all but two of Canada's sixteen Nobel laureates conducted their research outside Canada. Foreign students, a prime source of innovation for the United States, are now finding Canadian universities an increasingly attractive venue for their studies.

Between 2000 and 2005, the U.S. world market share in cross-border post-secondary education dropped from 26.1% to 21.6%; Canada's grew from 2.2% to 2.8%, despite increased security reviews, and it continues on an upward trajectory.[21]

According to the Conference Board of Canada, Canadians do not value advanced degrees or elite institutions as much as we do in the United States, but Canadian employers expect graduates to show up "ready to work," from a school system that includes a heavier "skills development" curriculum than most other countries. There appears to be less emphasis on job-related training and life-long-learning opportunities in Canada. Nor is there the level of university-business research partnership that often spurs innovations in the United States. Canada registers only a slightly better score on attainment for adult Canadians considered disadvantaged, such as immigrants, mature workers, and Aboriginal people. All three areas have been targeted for improvement.

In the long run, Canada's approach to broad-access high-quality public education may well provide it with the sharpest competitive edge over the U.S. The OECD has announced plans to extend its basic learning and skills evaluation to the university level by 2010 to assess worker preparedness for the global economy more accurately. The Institute for Competitiveness and Prosperity has estimated that, if Canada continues to narrow its educational-attainment gap, productivity could be increased by C$1,800 per capita—the equivalent of adding C$60 billion to Canada's GDP, a figure that would not be subject to the fluctuations of the commodity market.

Conclusion: The Puck Doesn't Stop Here

In the global economy our countries skate on the same
"ice"—innovation, competition, and entrepreneurship, and
this puck is in active play.

The style of our two teams is very different. The United
States has an economic star system, with no salary caps and no
holds barred, always on the offensive, ever eager to take the
risky, even reckless, shot. Canada celebrates the team, empha-
sizes the whole group, has reserve bench strength, and plays,
at the moment, more defensively than the potential of the
team warrants.[22] Who is going to "win" by 2050. Right now,
according to the scoreboard, the United States is ahead, but
signs are that Canada is grooming a championship team.

As in hockey, the perennial economic-policy questions of
valuation and ownership have to be taken into account.
"Valuation is more than just championships" *Forbes* told us in
the story about the Leafs, and the owners help define the per-
sonality of the team.

Most economists, when comparing the performance and
prosperity of economies, use the gross domestic product (GDP)
as the standard measure and a succinct way to evaluate differences. GDP focuses on growth and accumulated wealth, things
(goods and services) to which a dollar value can be attached. It
does not capture intangibles, such as quality of life, leisure
time, or happiness. Nor does it indicate if the prosperity
gained with increased wealth is shared among a broad array
of stakeholders in a country or in a way that would gain more
stakeholders.[23]

The Most Problematic Factors for Doing Business—United States

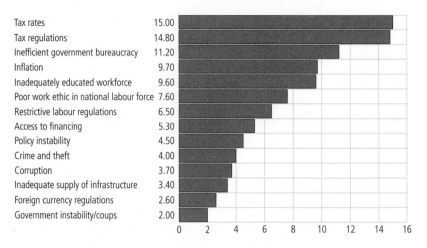

Factor	Value
Tax rates	15.00
Tax regulations	14.80
Inefficient government bureaucracy	11.20
Inflation	9.70
Inadequately educated workforce	9.60
Poor work ethic in national labour force	7.60
Restrictive labour regulations	6.50
Access to financing	5.30
Policy instability	4.50
Crime and theft	4.00
Corruption	3.70
Inadequate supply of infrastructure	3.40
Foreign currency regulations	2.60
Government instability/coups	2.00

The Most Problematic Factors for Doing Business—Canada

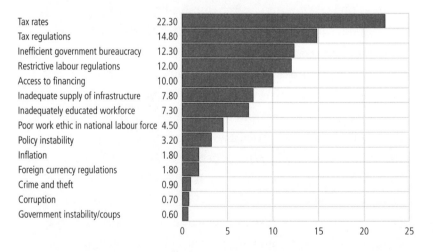

Factor	Value
Tax rates	22.30
Tax regulations	14.80
Inefficient government bureaucracy	12.30
Restrictive labour regulations	12.00
Access to financing	10.00
Inadequate supply of infrastructure	7.80
Inadequately educated workforce	7.30
Poor work ethic in national labour force	4.50
Policy instability	3.20
Inflation	1.80
Foreign currency regulations	1.80
Crime and theft	0.90
Corruption	0.70
Government instability/coups	0.60

Appears with permission of the World Economic Forum

CAN CANADA BE AS INNOVATIVE, COMPETITIVE, AND ENTREPRENEURIAL AS THE UNITED STATES?

An increasing number of serious American economists— as well as the 2008 U.S. presidential contenders—are beginning to voice concerns that an exclusive focus on growth and wealth is not sufficient to meet the current challenges of the New Economy. Inequalities of opportunity and access to education, health, and security in retirement are a keen concern for the future. "Ownership society" for one side vests in individual responsibility and choice; for the other, "ownership" represents a social compact individuals make with their governments. Both sides agree that "smart" economic policy ("smart" taxation, and "smart" regulation) facilitates the drivers of market growth and establishes confidence and trust in investors, the economy as a whole, and its public stakeholders. Hockey has messy pileups, but it also has rules of the game.

The 2007–08 Economist Intelligence Unit predicts that Canada will have made sufficient improvement in its business environment by 2012 to outrank the United States as one of the best places to do business. The U.S., which tumbled in the present report to its lowest ranking since the survey began in 1997, will, according to this report, still be stagnating from financial and macroeconomic risks, increased protectionism, security concerns, and bruised international relations. Fundamental features of the U.S.'s business environment— deregulated labour markets, good infrastructure, and leadership in technology—will keep the U.S. near the top of the league with only small differences among the countries at the top of the league. The global business environment will be good despite the U.S.'s fall from favour. According to the report, global GDP growth—including Canada's—will slow in the period between 2008 and 2012, but globalization will not be derailed. Although there will be limited progress in international trade liberalization, foreign trade and exchange regimes will continue to be freer, and labour and product markets will continue halting reform.[24]

Denmark, which took third spot on the World Economic Forum's Global Competitiveness Index, took top spot for the Economist Intelligence Unit's 2012 forecast for "its efficient markets, flexible labor markets and the quality of its goods and education." Denmark, the EIU observed "stands out for the successful balance that it appears to have struck between state and the market." The designer of the World Economic Forum's Competitiveness Index echoed this sentiment, saying its rankings had shown, "We should be talking about what government does, and not its size."[25]

What this tells us is that a convergence in American and Canadian "values" is probably not to our advantage in seeking the best public policies. Perhaps the greatest contribution we make to each other, with our differing philosophies and personalities—and even goals—is to provide a shifting blend of challenge and support, complementing and simultaneously competing with one another. Certainly a truism in sport is that when you play against someone better, your own game tends to improve.

Canada's choice to gauge itself against the United States is important in improving the prospects of not just Canadian but also American competitiveness. We need to watch and learn from each other over these next years, so that together, with our other partner, Mexico, we make North America a more competitive unit within the global economy. Despite the occasional outbreaks of "de-coupling" rhetoric, the United States and Canada have, and will continue to have, integrated economies and societies. Intrafirm trade within trans-border companies accounts for more than a third of U.S.–Canada trade, and the percentage is growing. Our two countries will increasingly define competitiveness as a function of cooperation and collaboration in what we do and make together. Perhaps we should view ourselves in a high-powered, but friendly, neighbourhood pick-up game in which we are refining our skills for global competition.

In 2050, the most important thing will be to ensure that the puck is still in active play between us, ideally with our great teams going end-to-end together with the rest of the world in a competition that is not merely an exhibition game.

This year McMaster University undergraduates in Hamilton, Ontario, won the U.S. Collegiate Inventors Competition. Wonder what that won–lost record will be in 2050?[26]

NOTES

1.   Nathan Vardi, "Winning Isn't Everything," *Forbes.com*, November 26, 2007. http://members.forbes.com/forbes/2007/1126/096.html (accessed November 14, 2007). See also, *Wall Street Journal*, "Despite Bankruptcy on Ice, Maple Leafs Shine Financially," November 9, 2007, p. B5.

2. Enterprise value is the market value of a business's equity, plus its interest-bearing debt, minus its cash equivalents.

3. The World Economic Forum, *The Global Competitiveness Report, 2007-2008*. See also, International Institute for Management Development (IMB) Business School's *2007 World Competitiveness Scoreboard* See also, C.D. Howe Institute commentary by Peter Howitt, "Innovation, Competition and Growth: A Schumpeterian View on Canada's Economy." See also, Gideon Rachman, "For Nations, Small Is Beautiful," *Financial Times*, December 3, 2007. See also, *Time* magazine's coverage on the Global Competitiveness Index results at www.time.com/globalbusiness.
See also, Chris Giles, "U.S. Tops Global Competitiveness Index," *Financial Times*, October 31, 2007.
See also, "U.S. Regains Status as the World's Most Competitive Economy," *International Herald Tribune*, October 31, 2007.

4. "America's Vulnerable Economy," *The Economist*, November 17, 2007. See also, Peter S. Goodman, "Trying to Guess What Happens Next," *New York Times*, November 25, 2007.

5. Paul Krugman, "Innovating Our Way to Financial Crisis," *New York Times*, December 3, 2007.

6. Statistical data and other information for this portion of the essay has been extracted from the following reports (the data cited in these reports is in purchasing power parity terms):
"How Canada Performs: A Report Card on Canada," June 2007. Conference Board of Canada;
"Agenda for Canada's Prosperity," Institute for Competitiveness and Prosperity;
The Canada Project, The Conference Board of Canada;
One Issue Two Voices, The Canada Institute at the Woodrow Wilson

International Center for Scholars.

Also see *Maclean's* magazine's exclusive reports:

"How to Fix Canada—On the Brink";

"How to Fix Canada—Letting It Go to Waste";

"How to Fix Canada—Bright Lights, Big Problems."

7. "How Canada Performs: A Report Card on Canada," June 2007. Page
    64. Conference Board of Canada.

    See also, Someshwar Rao, Jianmin Tang, and Weimin Wang,
    "Productivity Levels Between Canadian and U.S. Industries,"
    International Productivity Monitor, Number 9, Fall 2004, Micro-
    Economic Policy Analysis Branch, Industry Canada.

8. Shawn McCarthy, "Bank of Canada Will Respond to Global
    Turbulence: Dodge," *Globe and Mail*, November 17, 2007.

    See also, "Liftoff a Long Time Coming," collection of articles.
    Financial Post, September 22, 2007.

    See also, "Living with a Strong Loonie," *National Post*, September 22, 2007.

    See also, Joe Brean, "Dear Diary: Loonie," *National Post*, September
    22, 2007.

    See also, "A new low: The Dollar in Free Fall," Nov. 4-10, *New York
    Times*, November 11, 2007. See also "Loonie Jumps a U.S. Cent," *thes-
    tar.com*, November 16, 2007.

    See also, David Olive, "Soaring Loonie a Warning in Disguise," *thes-
    tar.com*, October 28, 2007.

    See also, Remarks by Paul Jenkins, Senior Deputy Governor of the
    Bank of Canada to the Canadian Association of New York. "North
    America in Today's Global Economic Setting," November 6, 2007.

    See also, William Watson, "Sink the Loonie!" *Financial Post*,
    September 21, 2007.

9. Public Broadcasting System (PBS) Report, "Midwest Manufacturers
    Fight to Stay in Global Marketplace," Online News Hour. See also

Konrad Yakabuski "It Ain't Pretty," *Globe and Mail*, November 29, 2007. See also Greg Keenan, "In One Town Boom. In Another, Gloom," *Globe and Mail*, November 30, 2007.

10. Statistics are taken from the following three reports:
"How Canada Performs: A Report Card on Canada," June 2007. Conference Board of Canada.
Agenda for Canada's Prosperity, Institute for Competitiveness and Prosperity.
The Canada Project, The Conference Board of Canada.

11. One recent comparative review of the two educational systems suggests that factors unrelated to the educational system could account for better student performance, i.e., "Canada doesn't have the same problems with notorious socio-economically disadvantaged neighborhoods ... the same kind of racial tension ... a large population of uneducated immigrants." See David Jones and David Kilgour, "Uneasy Neighbors: Canada, the USA and the Dynamics of State, Industry and Culture," p. 112. John Wiley & Sons Canada, Ltd.

12. "How Canada Performs: A Report Card on Canada," p. 83, June 2007 Conference Board of Canada.

13. 2007 OECD in Figures, pp. 50–51. *Education at a Glance—OECD Indicators 2006*, OECD, Paris, 2006.

14. OECD 2003 Programme for International Student Assessment (PISA). Canada's mean score placed it 7th in math to the U.S.'s 28th ranking, 3rd in reading to the U.S.'s 18th, 11th in science to the U.S.'s 22nd; and 9th in problem-solving to the U.S.'s 29th.
Results of the PISA 2006 survey will be released on December 4, 2007, after the submission of this essay. Also see *Trends in Mathematics and Science Survey* (TIMSS). A new study by Gary Phillips at the American

Institute of Research entitled "Chance Favors the Prepared Mind:
Mathematics and Science Indicators for Comparing States and
Nations" does not include Canadian data. It suggests that American
students in low-performing states like Alabama do better in math and
science than students in most foreign countries, but that students in
high-performing Asian competitor countries significantly outperform
American students in high-achieving states like Massachusetts in math
and North Dakota for science. See also, National Center for Education
Statistics, U.S. Department of Education, "Dropout Rates in the
United States: 2005" (June 2007). http://nces.ed.gov/Pubsearch/pub-
sinfo.asp?pubid=2007059 (accessed January 7, 2008).

15. Canadian Education Statistics Council (CESC), *Education Indicators in
Canada: Report of the Pan-Canadian Education Indicators Program (PCEIP)
2007*, http://www.statcan.ca/english/freepub/81-582-XIE/81-582-XIE
2007001.htm (accessed January 7, 2008).

16. Mike Baker, "Schools Face Up to Global Leagues," BBC News website.
See also, Sam Dillon, "Study Compares States' Math and Sciences
Scores with Other Countries," *New York Times*, November 14, 2007. See
also, "Bright Sparks," *The Economist*, February 8, 2007. See also, June
Kronholz, "Economic Time Bomb: U.S. Teens Are Among the Worst
at Math," *The Wall Street Journal*. December 7, 2007.

17. John M. Bridgeland, John J. Dilulio, Jr., and Karen Burke Morison,
"The Silent Epidemic: Perspectives of High School Dropouts," report
by Civic Enterprises in association with Peter D. Hart Research
Associates for the Bill & Melinda Gates Foundation (March 2006).
http://www.gatesfoundation.org/nr/downloads/ed/TheSilentEpid
emic3-06FINAL.pdf (accessed January 7, 2008).

18. OECD 2002 Higher Education and Adult Learning, Education at a
Glance. http://www.oecd.org/linklist/0,3435,en_2649_39263238_

2735794_1_1_1_1,00.html#39324034 (accessed January 7, 2008). David S. Broder, "The Dropout Challenge," *The Washington Post*, February 26, 2006. See also, Robert Balfanz and John Bridgeland, "A Plan to Fix 'Dropout Factories,'" *Christian Science Monitor*, November 23, 2007.

19. *Times* Higher Education Supplement http://www.thes.co.uk/world rankings/ (accessed December 3, 2007). See also, Shanghai Jiao Tong University's university rankings, http://ed.sjtu.edu.cn/ranking.htm (accessed December 3, 2007).

20. Institute of International Education. *Open Doors Report 2007*. The majority of Canadians are at the undergraduate (47.9%) and graduate level (44.2%). Breakdown not available for Americans studying in Canada. http://opendoors.iienetwork.org/ (accessed December 3, 2007).

21. *The Economist*, "Measuring Mortarboards," November 17, 2007. See also, "The Dangerous Wealth of the Ivy League," *Businessweek*, November 29, 2007. See also, Fen Osler Hampson and Alex Mackenzie, "Why Is Canadian Science on the Nobel Sidelines?" *Globe and Mail*, November 30, 2007. See also, "Mobilizing Science and Technology to Canada's Advantage," Industry Canada, May 2007.

22. This image tracks closely the distinction Seymour Martin Lipset drew between our two countries: Canadian values emphasize the community and trust in the government to act in the public interest for the public good, as embodied in the technical phrase "peace, order, and good government." American values emphasize the individual and the suspicion of government as embodied in the Declaration of Independence to allow for "life, liberty and the pursuit of happiness." See Seymour Martin Lipset, "American Exceptionalism: A Double-Edged Sword," W.W. Norton & Company, April 1997. See also, Seymour Lipset, "Historical Traditions and National Characteristics," *Canadian Journal of Sociology* (Summer 1986): 128. See also by

Seymour Lipset, "Continental Divide: The Values and Institutions of the United States and Canada," (New York: Routledge, 1990). See also, Patrick James and Mark Kasoff, "Canadian Studies in the New Millennium" (University of Toronto Press, 2008). See also, Northrop Frye, "Divisions on a Ground: Essays on Canadian Culture" (Anansi: Toronto, 1982).

23. Ryan Macdonald, "Canadian and U.S. Real Income Growth Pre and Post 2000: A Reversal of Fortunes," *Economic Analysis Research Paper Series*, Statistics Canada. This study finds that Canada performs better than the U.S. on relative per capita performance when terms of trade and international income flows are incorporated into a traditional GDP per capita growth based analysis. The study conceded however, that the commodity boom has buoyed the figures and that their approach is an alternative interpretation. See also, Lawrence Summers, "Harness Market Forces to Share Prosperity," *Financial Times*, June 24, 2007. See also, Eduardo Porter, "All They Are Saying Is Give Happiness a Chance," *New York Times*, November 12, 2007. See also, "World Economic Outlook October 2007," International Monetary Fund. See also, Eric Weiner, "Actually, Happiness Isn't Within," *The Christian Science Monitor*, January 7, 2008.

24. "Business Environment Rankings: Outpacing America," *The Economist*, October 29, 2007.

25. See Barbara Kiviat, "Best Countries for Global Business," *Time*, November 15, 2007.

26. Daniel Girard, "McMaster Student Wins Invention Award," *thestar.com*, November 5, 2007.

OUR SHARED URBAN FUTURE

BY JOEL KOTKIN

WHILE THE LATE URBANIST JANE JACOBS may have moved to Toronto to protest the Vietnam War, she also inadvertently perpetuated the notion, popular on both sides of the border, that Canada's cities were intrinsically better run, more humane and more urban than those in the United States.

Jacobs, who chose to become a Canadian citizen, often railed against the massive suburbanization and urban decay that gripped America's cities in the decades between the 1970s and 1990s. In Toronto she saw "the most hopeful and healthy city in North America, still unmangled, still with options."

Such critiques of America only solidified her iconic status among Canadians. This is not surprising in a country whose intellectual elites have long considered the United States, as H.F. Angus wrote in the 1938 book *Canada and Her Great Neighbour*, "as a source of undesirable cultural and social influences." Canadian scholars frequently have regarded their urban culture as superior to that of their southern neighbour. Canadian cities, noted the influential University of Toronto sociologist S.D. Clark, lacked the "same corrupting influences" that proliferated in the United States.[1]

Yet as Jacobs reached her seventies and eighties, she also

seemed more clear-eyed in understanding that there were more commonalities than differences in what she called "our North American civilization." As in the United States, Canada's cities—most particularly Toronto—increasingly began to resemble the sprawling, auto-dependent, multi-centred metropolises she abhorred.[2]

A look at the trends suggests the increasing congruence of urban development patterns. Suburbanization is just the most obvious example. Today more than half of Toronto's population lives outside the expanded city limits or the megacity created in 1997, and the expansion of population continues apace in the periphery. Between 2001 and 2006 the growth rate for the expanded Toronto municipality was less then 1 per cent, or 22,000 people, while that of the suburban fringe was well above 18 per cent, or over 400,000. American demographer Wendell Cox devilishly calls Canada's premier city "the Los Angeles of the North."

A similar process of decentralization has occurred eco-nomically as well. According to a recent study by Aleem Kanji at the Toronto Board of Trade, the region has added 742,000 jobs since 1989, while the city's employment base has actually decreased by 54,000. The City of Toronto's overall economic output in the same time grew at less than one-fifth the rate of the region, and trailed Canada's and Ontario's by better than 50 per cent.

Much the same can be said of other Canadian cities, par-ticularly the older ones. The historic city of Montreal, for example, hit its peak population in 1971, and has continued to sprawl outwards. Between 1981 and 2001, the city's population, even with expanded borders, grew by a mere 3 per cent, while the suburbs of its inner ring expanded by nearly 50 per cent and of its outer ring, now extending to the Laurentians, by 75 per cent. This same pattern can be seen in Ottawa and Vancouver, as well as in booming Calgary, with most growth taking place disproportionately in the suburban outreaches.[3]

Canada's cities also share many of the same social and political problems as their American counterparts. There is growing concern about rising crime—once written off as a peculiarity of American cities—particularly in Montreal, Vancouver, and Toronto. And, as in America, much of the urban infrastructure appears to be increasingly in tatters.[4]

At the same time, Canadian cities are also experiencing a shift in traditional hierarchies, much as has occurred in the United States. Since the 1970s there has been a shift in power away from established centres—notably Montreal—and towards fast-growing areas in the west, like Calgary and Edmonton. It may not be accurate to call these northerly cities part of a fast-growing "sunbelt," as in the United States, but they are part of a dramatic movement away from more traditional transit-oriented dense cities to new, sprawling centres based almost exclusively on the automobile. Calgary, for example, has less than half as many residents per kilometre than does Toronto; Edmonton is nearly a third less dense.[5]

Important Differences

Despite these growing similarities, American and Canadian cities are not without their significant differences. For example, in the 1960s and 1970s, Canadian cities did not decline in the precipitous manner of their American counterparts. The reasons for this vary, having much to do with a colder climate, which serves to promote denser development, as well as the far more powerful influence of the national and provincial governments over land use.

But perhaps the most critical divergence has been sociological. Unlike American cities, Canadian urban areas did not have to cope with the sad legacy of slavery. In the decades following Emancipation, particularly starting in the early 1900s, millions of African Americans—most of them poorly educated—flocked into American cities.

"When you look at the biggest difference between Canadian and American cities it is two hundred years of slavery and its effects," notes Wendell Cox, who studied demographic trends in both countries extensively.

Although their conditions improved over their miserable experience in the South, the new African American residents of the U.S.A.'s great northern and Midwestern industrial cities faced considerable discrimination and hardship. And tragically, even as they began to assert their rights and political influence, the national economy began rapidly to both de-industrialize and decentralize.

This left African Americans in the majority in many cities—Detroit, St. Louis, Oakland, Cleveland, Philadelphia, Newark, Baltimore—at the very time that their traditional economic base was being undermined. By the 1960s they found themselves in a precarious position, with many essentially relying on government assistance or employment to sustain themselves.

These created widely divergent realities between American and Canadian cities. The social dislocations spurred rapid out-migration of whites to the suburbs, and with them many businesses. The loss of jobs and the pent-up frustrations among African Americans created a death spiral marked by occasional riots, rising crime, and the creation of what were often anti-business black-nationalist governments in many cities. By 1968, the Kerner Commission spoke of "two Americas," one black and urban, the other white and suburban.

By 1990, even New Yorkers seemed to have lost their faith in the cult of urban grandiosity; roughly six in ten told surveyors that they would live somewhere else if they could.[6] But the greatest declines took place in the old industrial cities—St. Louis, Cleveland, Detroit—which a century earlier had stood at the cutting edge of urban development.[7]

For their part, Canadian cities never suffered this scale of social disaster. Nor have they had to cope with anything like the sort of mass migration from south of the border that has occurred in the United States, creating a new spike in poverty-stricken populations in many cities, particularly in the American Southwest. To be sure, this immigrant wave has brought many positives to American cities, but the presence of a large, often ill-educated, population in the urban cores has intensified the social and economic gap between urban and suburban America.

The Universal Aspiration: America As Vanguard

Yet despite these differences, Canadian and American cities shared one overwhelming similarity—the rise of suburbia.

Rather than being a peculiarity of the American "way of life," as is often asserted by Canadian and other critics, the shift to suburbia appears to be a prevailing characteristic of advanced urban civilizations everywhere in the world.

Compared to the option of living closely packed in apartment blocks, most human beings seemed to define their personal "better city" in terms of a little more space and privacy, and perhaps even a spot of lawn. Noted prominent Los Angeles urbanist and Italian immigrant Edgardo Contini:

> The suburban house is the idealization of every immigrant's dream—the vassal's dream of his own castle. Europeans who come here are delighted by our suburbs. Not to live in an apartment! It is a universal aspiration to own your own home.[8]

These same patterns can be seen everywhere, including places like Europe, where land is scarcer and energy more expensive than in North America[9]—even in Paris, arguably the world's most magnificently planned dense urban centre.[10] Tokyo, the world's largest city and a place with a superb mass-transit system, has also expanded outward in dramatic fashion. Forced to the periphery to find affordable homes, almost ten million people settled in the suburban regions around the main cities of the Kanto plain between 1970 and 1995.[11]

A similar pattern can also be seen in Great Britain. Between 1980 and 2000, the built-up area of Britain more than doubled, even though the rate of population growth was slight.[12] Perhaps more revealing, some 70 per cent of those still dwelling in the urban centres in 2000 told surveyors that they would prefer living somewhere else.[13]

Of course, many critics assign the blame for this worldwide trend on the United States. And indeed, in terms of mass suburbanization, America was first, in large part because, following the Second World War, it was the only country that possessed the financial wherewithal to construct homes on a massive basis. The pent-up demand was insatiable: the country had gone for nearly fifteen years with little residential building and a historically low birth rate. Then that birthrate began to rise at one of the highest rates in U.S. demographic history.

This led to a remarkable quickening of the pace of suburbanization in America which accounted for a remarkable 84 per cent of the nation's population increase during the 1950s. Aided by the passage of legislation to aid veterans, home ownership became a common expectation for the middle, and even the working, classes. By the mid-1980s, America enjoyed a rate of home-ownership that encompassed roughly two thirds of all families, double that of such prosperous countries as Germany, Switzerland, France, Great Britain, and Norway. Nearly three-quarters of AFL-CIO members and the vast majority of intact families owned their own homes.[14]

This suburban wave was made possible by remarkable innovations in home building that today are often widely castigated by social critics, architects, and planners. New developments such as Levittown, which arose out on the Long Island flatlands in the late 1940s and early 1950s,[15] used mass production techniques that developer William Levitt learned while serving in the U.S. Navy. He put his challenge succinctly:

"Any damned fool can build homes. What counts is how many you can sell for how little."[16]

New York planning czar (and one of Jane Jacobs's great villains) Robert Moses, who helped plan the road system that made developments like Levittown viable, understood the enormous appeal of these new communities:

> The little identical suburban boxes of average people, which differ only in color and planting, represent a measure of success unheard of by hundreds of millions on other continents. Small plots reflect not merely the rapacity of developers but the caution of owners who do not want too much grass to cut and snow to shovel—details too intimate for historians.[17]

The suburbs, noted historian Jon C. Teaford, provided more than an endless procession of lawns and carports, but also "a mixture of escapism and reality."[18] They offered welcome respite, both from crowded urban neighbourhoods and old ethnic ties. There one could make new friendships and associations without worrying about old social conventions. And, with their ample yards, new schools and parks, the novelist Ralph G. Martin noted that the suburbs seem to offer "a paradise for children."[19]

Suburb As Anti City

Like many urbanists, Jane Jacobs was particularly hostile both to suburbia and its primary means of transportation, the car.

She identified the automobile as "the chief destroyer" of American communities; she did not consider the new living places made possible by the car to be "communities" in the manner of the dense Manhattan communities she lionized.[20]

This view has been particularly popular among planners and architects, many of whom otherwise disagreed with Jacobs's opposition to top-down solutions to urban problems. "Hell," declared a 1957 article in *Community Planning Review*, "is a suburb." Suburbia, wrote architecture critic Ana Louise Huxtable, presented a picture of "cliché conformity as far as the eye could see."

This disdain among the intellectuals often extended to the suburbanites themselves. Herbert Gans, a student of Lewis Mumford and later a professor at Columbia University in Manhattan, took a contrarian and more benign view of suburbs. In his *The Levittowners*, he refers to suburbanites as "an uneducated, gullible, petty 'mass' which rejects the culture that would make it fully human." The suburbanite displeased "the professional planner and the intellectual defender of cosmopolitan culture."

This critique became even more widespread with the rise of the counterculture in the 1960s. Suburbia was seen as one of many "tasteless travesties of mass society," along with fast and processed food, plastics, and large cars. It represented the opposite of the hip urban scene; Paul Knox, former dean of the College of Architecture and Urban Studies at Virginia Tech in Blacksburg, Virginia, even labelled suburbs as "vulgaria."[21]

More recently, new urbanism—with its espousal of a greater reliance on walkways, mixed uses, and diverse levels of residential development—has added to the critique of sub-urbia, even while presenting often-helpful suggestions about making it more intimate and human in scale. Many adherents of new urbanism are also fundamentally hostile to backyards, cul-de-sacs, and single-family houses, those things that are often favoured by families to provide safety, privacy, and play-grounds for their children.[22]

Suburbia's most extreme critics include author James Howard Kunstler, a figure widely revered among new urban-ists, who portrays the suburban lifestyle in much the way an early Christian might have described classical Rome: "I begin to come to the conclusion that we Americans are these days a wicked people who deserve to be punished." Kunstler openly "gloats" over the prospect that high energy prices will lead to the demise of the very places where most Americans live.[23]

Following the recent controversy over global warming and its causes, suburbia has once again been made a culprit—this time for a worldwide environmental disaster. Advocates of "smart growth," along with some environmental activists, suggest that energy-related problems and global warming necessitate policies that will promote dense communities ori-ented not around automobiles, but around mass transit.

Canadian Realities: Laval and Montreal; Markham and Toronto

Many Canadian environmentalists, social commentators, and urbanists, like their American counterparts, are full of invective for suburbanization. Some take comfort from Kunstler's notion that, as consultant Richard Gilbert puts it, "suburban life as we know it could be doomed," the victim of high energy prices.

Gilbert suggests that banks will soon abandon suburbs—except those near transit stops—as people flock back to the city.[24] Other Jeremiads from Canadian sources maintain that suburbs are also bad for families (notwithstanding the fact that families overall keep heading for the periphery) and are inimical to what one critic called the country's "decline in community and sense of civic commitment."[25]

Perhaps the most notable recent entry in the anti-suburban vein has been the recent Canadian documentary by filmmaker Gary Burns. *Radiant City* mocked suburban life and won widespread plaudits on both sides of the border. The documentary shows numerous clippings of anti-suburban guru Kunstler and follows a family, the Mosses, through their allegedly empty suburban lives.

Like their American counterparts, Canadian critics portray suburbs as anti-democratic and intolerant. Ironically, as one reviewer noted, Burns's movie is a "monologue," with no one speaking in defence of suburbia and with many of the real-life interviews scripted (as it later turned out). Nevertheless, not surprisingly, the Canadian urban press loved it, with one reviewer finding it "funny in a shuddery kind of way."[26]

Yet, as social critics fulminate, Canadians themselves continue to clamour for this American-style dystopia. And suburbia is not just for the clueless dummies, as is often suggested by the urban press. In fact, despite highly promoted urban "tech" centres in cities such as Toronto, the focal point for Canada's high-end economic growth has been in the far reaches of cities like Waterloo, the Toronto suburb of Markham, and on the suburban fringes of Ottawa.[27]

This process also can be seen in Montreal, Canada's greatest traditional city. Despite its enormous charm, Montreal's middle class and its high-tech industry have been migrating out of town to less-storied places like Laval, a burgeoning suburban town directly to the north.

Like most of Quebec, Laval, until very recently, was primarily an agricultural area, dotted by small villages founded largely in the eighteenth century. Many of these communities, such as Sainte-Rose, remain discernible as places with unique characteristics. Saint Vincent-de-Paul and Saint-Martin also have long histories as independent communities. Even today Laval has more than 1,800 buildings that are over one hundred years old.[28]

As Montreal stagnated, both demographically and economically, Laval grew from a small town with a few thousand rural inhabitants to a classic suburban bedroom community with two hundred thousand residents by 1967. Since then, the area has continued to grow far more rapidly— both economically and demographically—than Montreal. Between 1981 and 2001, for example, Laval gained some eighty-six thousand residents, while the pre-2002 Montreal gained fifty-two thousand. Laval's growth rate was 32 per cent, almost ten times that of Montreal.[29]

In many ways, the appeal of Laval is consistent with patterns seen in many high-tech areas in the United States. In a study I conducted with Remy Tremblay at the University of Quebec, entrepreneurs and residents explained the advantages of locating in Laval compared to Montreal. One prominent reason was crime: the homicide rate in Laval is far below that of the rest of Quebec.[30]

Perhaps more important, however, was the city's modern auto-oriented infrastructure. As Normand de Montigny, executive director of the Quebec Biotechnology Innovation Centre, headquartered in Laval, suggests:

> Laval is very well positioned in the greater Montreal area.... Laval has the infrastructure that has built up over twenty years. They bought the land and set it aside for the industry. There is a lot of cohesion here and we have access to the capabilities of business in Montreal.

Other Laval businesspeople cited another key advantage of Laval—its suburban, family-friendly quality of life. Pierre Pelletier, chef de division planification et amenagement du territoire for the Laval Service de L'Urbanisme, traces this in large part to the city's largely "low density" residential structure, its good schools, and low rate of crime. Normand de Montigny feels that many high-tech experts underestimate the importance of this family-friendly environment:

> Laval is for families and when you think about companies and employees, you have to think not just about economics or even businesses or companies. You have to think of the families who make up the companies.

Emerging Changes In the Urban Hierarchy

Laval reflects one large piece of the urban future—one whose epicentre will increasingly be located on the suburban frontier. But this is only part of the unfolding story. Whether in Canada or America, the history of cities has a protean character, and there will be shifts in the relative importance of cities within the national—and by extension the global—system of cities, as well as in the geographic layout of metropolitan areas.

In many ways, these developments are related. In America, as well as Canada, the secular trend has been away from traditional dense cities—Montreal, Chicago, San Francisco—and towards the new frontier represented by "sprawl" cities. In America, this trend has been represented in the past most notably by Los Angeles, but more recently the most dramatic growth has taken place in previously "second tier" metropolitan areas such as Atlanta, Houston, Dallas, and Phoenix.

This same pattern can be seen in the Canadian shift towards cities such as Calgary and Edmonton, which has been furthered by the rising price of energy. Although environmentalists always suggest high energy prices will be of most help to traditional, transit-oriented cities, the experience of the 1970s, and of the last few years, has been that it is the energy-producing cities—Houston in the United States, Calgary and Edmonton in Canada—that are the major beneficiaries. In 2005 alone, for example, over forty thousand people migrated from other provinces to Albertan cities.[31]

These boomtowns—like their American cousins—have taken advantage of growth to keep their taxes low and attract new investors. This makes them fearsome national competitors even to Toronto, whose leaders now fear that they, like Montreal in the 1970s, will experience a movement of talent and firms, this time to urban Alberta.[32]

With their growing wealth, these new urban centres, following the pattern of cities throughout history, will begin to take on the trappings of cosmopolitan centres. Once overwhelmingly native-born, nearly one in five residents of Calgary are now foreign-born, with the United Kingdom, China, India, the Philippines, and Vietnam as the major contributors.[33] And Calgary, with Canada's highest per capita GDP, now has something of a night life, as it attracts the best and brightest from across both Canada and the world.[34]

Such a competitive environment, both within and between cities, may seem unsettling to Canadians, yet it is as much a part of their history as it is America's. Urban centres of gravity have always shifted with changes in technology—railroads, airplanes, cars, the Internet—and markets. Alberta's ascendency, like Houston's, will ride with the rising price of energy and resources; the distance between these cities and national, as well as world, markets are also increasingly telescoped by technology. Calgary and Edmonton, like Houston or Phoenix, are no longer on the fringes of the world city system, but are emerging players within it.

The Rise of Suburban Villages
In a similar way, the inexorable movement towards decentralization will change the nature of the expanding suburban periphery that has developed around all major Canadian cities.

With the growth of technology and high-end business services in the suburbs, such as those outside Toronto,[35] it is likely we will see the growth of cultural and recreational facilities and sophisticated shopping in these places.

In the United States, we can already see this in the evolution of suburban "villages," like the Woodlands, outside Houston, or Valencia, north of Los Angeles. In these and many other places, the critical mass of suburban industry and population has engendered the growth of cultural and economic "centres" that approximate in their own way the traditional functions of the urban core.

This pattern is just evolving in Vancouver. Its suburbs, such as Richmond, have developed into business, as well as cultural, hubs, particularly for the expanding Asian market. Other Canadian suburban cities—such as Mississauga, Kanata, and Markham, as well as Laval—have all made considerable investments to enhance their central districts, sometimes drawing on the entrepreneurial energies of their burgeoning immigrant populations.[36]

This is increasingly clear both to suburban political leaders and businessmen. The development of local cultural institutions, the revivification of older commercial areas, as well as the building of bike trails, parks, and other recreational amenities, for example, could further enhance the quality of life in these "villages" and sharpen their competitive advantages against the core cities and their suburban rivals.

A New Future for Traditional Cores?

At the same time, the traditional cores will seek strategies to cope with their relative decline as economic and demographic centres. One strategy will be to rely increasingly on entertainment, art, tourism, and media to sustain their economy. And while they seem resigned to losing families and upwardly mobile immigrants to the suburbs, they hope to make up for some of these losses by attracting well-educated young people, singles, and some wealthier childless couples.

This approach has its limitations. In cities with a culturally based focus, there is often strong growth in the urban core, with high-end condominiums and sometimes clusters of students. But this often does not make up for the loss of population in surrounding neighbourhoods that traditionally housed middle-class families, including urbanites entering their thirties. This pattern can already be seen clearly in such U.S. cities as San Francisco, Boston, and Seattle, as well as in large swaths of New York, Chicago, Philadelphia, and Los Angeles.

As a result, even as their cores gentrify admirably, many of these cities have experienced below-average job growth and significant out-migration. On some levels, those of amenities, culture, and residential development, they performed well, particularly in the early millennial housing "bubble," but in terms of traditional measurements, such as overall economic growth, social mobility, and population increase, their performance tends to be mediocre to poor.[37]

This pattern can also be seen in Canadian cities. Both central Toronto and Montreal have seen significant increases in residents in their cores, but relative stagnation in their neighbourhoods.

The economic base, as in the United States, has shifted as these cities rely more and more on the culture-based industries and tourism to sustain their economies. Both have dabbled in Richard Florida's "creative class" theory, which promotes culture-based industry and urban bohemianism as the *summum bonum* of the post-industrial society.[38]

The resulting social mix is often problematic. Some cities display many of the problems associated with "ephemeral cities" like San Francisco. Cities with a "creative" focus often feel they can follow a tax and regulatory regime detrimental to those industries that traditionally provided upward mobility and employment to the working classes. Montreal, notes Elliot Lifson, vice-chairman of Peerless Clothing, North America's largest suit manufacturer, treats with "indifference" companies such as his, which employ tens of thousand of skilled and semi-skilled workers, many of them recent immigrants.[39]

In the Canadian context, this may be most evident in Vancouver, a city that is praised internationally for its strongly revived downtown core. Although over the past two decades, the city's downtown population has more than doubled, to a hundred thousand, its economic role has dissipated, as business continues to flock to the periphery. Nearly one-third of the city's office jobs have departed since 2000, leaving the city largely "a dormitory suburb," which people leave for the morning commute to the suburbs.

Ultimately, this changes the very nature of urbanism, replacing the model of the city as centre of aspiration with one that, as one observer puts it, is more focused on "validating lifestyle rather than creating wealth."[40] As the economy for the working and middle classes gets tougher due to rising costs and the migration of jobs, social problems such as crime, drug use, and homelessness—long associated with elite U.S. cities such as San Francisco—not surprisingly have emerged. Vancouver has its well-known drug problems, and Toronto has faced an unfamiliar crime wave. Even booming Calgary suffers a growing homeless population.[41]

The Urban Future

In the future, cities in both countries will likely take shape following two different patterns. One of these will see the suburbs and even exurbs evolving into increasingly self-sufficient communities, an archipelago of villages. This is where most people will live and work and spend much of their time. The other will see the continued movement among traditional cities to capitalize on their roles as centres of high culture, youthful bohemianism, tourism, and selected elite industries, notably media, entertainment, and probably a slice of high-end business services.

Such new divisions of metropolitan functions in both countries are not necessarily the result that many urbanists who cherish the traditional diversity and roles of urban centres—including this author—would ideally like to see. And there remains hope, if urban political and economic leaders shift direction, that urban neighborhoods—whether in Montreal, Toronto or other Canadian cities—can once again accommodate middle-class families and the aspiring working class. This will take a new perspective, one that focuses on "basics" like schools, public safety, parks, infra-structure, and diverse economic opportunities as well as community institutions such as churches, synogogues and mosques. This may not halt the continued shift to the periphery but it can allow great cities to retain their relevance and appeal for more than a slice of the metropolitan population.

NOTES

1. Jeffrey D. Brison, "Rockefeller, Carnegie and Canada: American Philanthropy and the Arts and Letters in Canada," McGill University Press (Montreal: 2005), p. 74.

2. "Influential Author Jane Jacobs Dies at Age 89," CTV.com, April 25, 2006; James Howard Kunstler and Jane Jacobs interview, www.kunstler.com for *Metropolis* Magazine, March 2001, interview September 6, 2000.

3. Demographia.com "Canada City Population History: Montreal, Ottawa, Toronto and Vancouver: Bringing Business Back to Toronto's Core," Toronto Board of Trade, September/October, interview with Aleem Kanji, Toronto Board of Trade; "The Montreal Region: Planning at Peace with the Future," *Demographia*, November 1, 2003; Wendell Cox, "Megacity Fallout," *Financial Post*, July 18. 2007.

4. "Taking a lesson from U.S. Inner Cities," *National Post*, March 13, 2006.

5. *Demographia*, "Canada and Western USA Urban Areas: Core and Suburban Density Analysis," based on 2000 Census.

6. Witold Rybczynski and Peter Linneman, "Shrinking Cites," *Wharton Real Estate Review* (Fall 1997); William Kornblum, "New York under Siege," in *The Other City: People and Politics in New York and London*, Humanities Press (Atlantic Highlands, New Jersey: 1995), p. 37; Jack Newfield and Paul du Brul, *The Abuse of Power: The Permanent Government and the Fall of New York*, Viking Press, (New York: 1977), pp. 18–24.

7. Kate Stohr, "Shrinking Cities Syndrome," *New York Times*, February 5, 2004; "London Comes Back to Life," *Economist*, November 9, 1996.

8. Jack Rosenthal, "The Outer City: An Overview of Suburban Turmoil in the United States," in Louis H. Masotti and Jeffrey K. Hadden, *Suburbia in Transition*, New Viewpoints, (New York: 1974) p. 269.

9. Manuel Valenzuela and Ana Olivera, "Madrid Capital City and metropolitan region," in Hugh Clout, editor, *Europe's Cities in the Late 20th Century*, Royal Dutch Geographical Society, (Utrecht: 1996), pp. 57–59; Gunther Glebe, "Dusseldorf: economic restructuring and demographic transformation," in High Clout, editor, *Europe's Cities in the Late 20th Century*, Royal Dutch Geographical Society, (Utrecht: 1996), pp. 126–132.

10. Martine Berger, "Trajectories in Living Space, Employment and Housing Stock: The Example of the Parisian Metropolis in the 1980s and 1990s," Blackwell Publishers, 1996; Alfred Fierro, *Historical Dictionary of Paris*, Scarecrow Press, (London: 1998), p. 19; Jean Robert, "Paris and the Ile de France: national capital, world city," in High Clout, editor, *Europe's Cities in the Late 20th Century*, Royal Dutch Geographical Society, (Utrecht: 1996), pp. 17–22.

11. Andre Sorensen, "Subcentres and Satellite Cities: Tokyo's 20th Century Experience of Planned Polycentrism," *International Planning Studies, Volume 6, No. 1, 9-32*, 2001; Richard Hill and Kuniko Fujita, "Japanese Cities in the World Economy," in *Japanese Cities in the World*

Economy, Temple University Press, (Philadelphia: 1993), p. 11; Edward Seidenstacker, *Tokyo Rising: The City Since the Great Earthquake*, Alfred Knopf, 1990, pp. 336–337.

12. Richard Rogers and Richard Burdett, "Let's Cram More Into the City," *New Statesman*, May 22, 2000.

13. Patrick Collinson, "Property: A Slowdown will mean a steadier market," *Guardian*, October 28, 2000; "The Music of the Metropolis," *Economist*, August 2, 1997.

14. Kenneth Jackson, *Crabgrass Frontier: The Suburbanization of the United States*, Oxford University Press, (New York: 1985), p. 7; Donaldson, *op. cit.*, p. 4.

15. Fred Siegel, *The Future Once Happened Here: New York, D.C., L.A., and the Fate of America's Big Cities, (uncorrected proof)*, Free Press; New York, 1997, p. x.

16. John Blackwell, "1951: American Dream Houses, all in a row," *The Trentonian*, October 22, 2007.

17. Robert Moses, "Are Cities Dead?," in C.E, Elias, Jr, James Gillies, Svend Riemer, editors, *Metropolis: Values in Conflict*, Wadworth Publishing, (Belmont, CA: 1965), p. 53.

18. Jon C. Teaford, *Post-Suburbia: Government and Politics in Edge Cities*, Johns Hopkins Press, (Baltimore: 1997), p. 10.

19. Ralph G. Martin, "A New Life Style," in Louis H. Masotti and Jeffrey K. Hadden, *Suburbia in Transition*, New Viewpoints, (New York: 1974), pp. 14–21; William H. Whyte, *The Organization Man*, Doubleday, (Garden City, New York: 1956), p. 331.

20. Jane Jacobs, *Dark Age Ahead*, Random House, (New York: 2004), p. 37.

21. Steven Hayward, "Legends of the Sprawl," *Policy Review*, September-October 1998; Thomas Frank, *The Conquest of Cool: Business Culture, Counterculture and the Rise of Hip Consumerism*, University of Chicago, (Chicago: 1997), p. 13; Paul Knox, "Vulgaria: The Re-enchantment of Suburbia," *Opolis*, Volume 1, issue 2, 2005.

22. Michael Southworth and Eran Ben Joseph, "Reconsidering the Cul-de-Sac," *Access*, Spring 2004, p. 31.

23. James Kunstler, "Remarks in Providence," October 19, 2001; James Kunstler, *Home From Nowhere, Coda: What I Live For*, Simon and Shuster (New York: 1996); James Kunstler, "Atlanta: Does Edge City Have a Future?," www.kunstler.com; James Howard Kunstler, Cluster_uck Nation, November 8, 2004.

24. Richard Gilbert, "Suburbs as we know them are doomed by the coming energy crunch," *Population Institute of Canada*, May 22, 2003.

25. Ryan McGreal, *Child and Youth Friendly Land-Use and Transport Planning Guidelines*, The Centre for Sustainable Transportation, March 28, 2005, Nina-Marie Lister, "Beyond Sprawl," *Alternatives Journal*, Summer 2000.

26. V.A. Musettom, "Keeping Up with the Zones on a tour of dehumanizing suburbia," *New York Post*, May 30, 2007; Grady Hendrix, "Pulling Weeds from the Suburban Dream," *New York Sun*, May 30, 2007; Geoff Pevere, *Toronto Star*, September 8, 2007.

27. Patricia Bailey, "Sprawling towards E-topia," *Ottawa Citizen*, September 26, 2000.

28. "Ville de Laval: Histoire et patromoine architectural," Ville de Laval, 1983.

29. "Montreal Region: Planning at Peace with the Future," *Demographia*, November 1, 2003.

30. QUALITÉ DE VIE LAVALLOISE, COMPÉTITIVITÉ ET «TALENTS» par Rémy Tremblay et Joel Kotkin, Cite de Laval, 2006.

31. "Best Cities for an oil crisis," CNN Money, March 24, 2006; US BLS data, 2006-7; Mary Anastasia O'Grady, "A Tale of Two Oil Patches," *Wall Street Journal*, June 16, 2006; source: Mary Axworthy, City of Calgary.

32. "Economic Outlook 2006-2011," City of Calgary, April 4, 2006, p. 18.

33. Bernard Simon, "Canada Looks West for Creative Energy," *Los Angeles Times*, February 27th, 2006.

34. Anne Kingston, "Swinging Calgary," *Maclean's*, March 28, 2006. 2–6.

35. David A. Kaplan, *The Silicon Boys and their Valley of Dreams*, William Morrow and Company, Inc. (New York), 1999, p. 13; Manuel Castells, *The Rise of the Network Society*, Blackwell Publishers, 1996, p. 48; "Cyber Cities," *Canadian Business*, June 12, 1998.

36. Patricia Bailey, "Sprawling towards E-topia," *Ottawa Citizen*, September 26, 2000.

37. Alan Berube and Benjamin Forman, "In-City Population Growth Occurs Near the Edge," Brookings Institution, November 16, 2005; analysis of population and economic trends prepared by Praxis Strategy Group.

38. Wendell Cox, "Megacity Fallout," *Financial Post*, July 18, 2007.

39. Elliot Lifson, "Industrial policy stacked against apparel industry," *Financial Post*, March 24, 2004; interview with author.

40. Trevor Brody, "Downtown's Last Resort," *Canadian Architect*, August 2006; Linda Baker, "The Zoning Policy That Worked Too Well," *New York Times*, January 17, 2007.

41. Jennifer S. Forsyth, "Oil Rich Calgary Finds Boomtimes Have a Downside," *Wall Street Journal*, August 30, 2006.

FURTHER READING

In addition to the works referenced in endnotes, the following titles have been cited in this collection.

Geneive Abdo, *Mecca and Main Street: Muslim Life in America After 9/11*. Oxford University Press (2007).

Michael Adams, *Fire and Ice: The United States, Canada and the Myth of Converging Values*. Penguin Books Canada (2003).

Saul Bellow, *Him with His Foot in His Mouth and Other Stories*. Harper Publishing (1984).

Jared Diamond, *Guns, Germs, and Steel*. W. W. Norton & Company (2005).

Nathan Glazer, *We Are All Multiculturalists Now*. Harvard University Press (1998).

Nathan Glazer and Daniel P. Moynihan, *Beyond the Melting Pot: The Negroes, Puerto Ricans, Jews, Italians, and Irish of New York City*. Harvard University Press (1963).

George Grant, *Lament for a Nation: The Defeat of Canadian Nationalism*. McClelland & Stewart (1965).

David Gratzer, *Code Blue: Reviving Canada's Health Care System*. ECW Press (1999).

Samuel P. Huntington, *Who Are We?: The Challenges to America's National Identity*. Simon & Schuster (2005).

Bernard-Henri Lévy, *American Vertigo*. Gibson Square Books Ltd (2008).

Ohsfeldt, Robert and John Schneider, *The Business of Health*. AEI Press (2006).

John Porter, *The Vertical Mosiac: An Analysis of Social Class and Power in Canada*. University of Toronto Press (1967).

AUTHOR BIOGRAPHIES

Andrew Cohen is a professor of journalism and international affairs at Carleton University in Ottawa. He is a bestselling author and an award-winning journalist, who writes a syndicated weekly column for CanWest newspapers. Among his books are *While Canada Slept: How We Lost Our Place in the World*, which was a finalist for the Governor General's Literary Award, and *The Unfinished Canadian: The People We Are*, from which this essay is adapted. In 2007–08, he was a Visiting Fellow at The Aspen Institute and the German Institute for International and Security Affairs in Berlin.

Andrew Coyne is National Editor of *Maclean's* magazine. Raised in Winnipeg, Mr. Coyne graduated with a B.A. in Economics and History from the University of Toronto and a Master's degree from the London School of Economics. He has been an editorial writer and columnist for the *National Post*, the *Globe and Mail*, and the Southam newspaper chain. His work has also appeared in a number of other publications in Canada and abroad, including the *New York Times*, the *Wall Street Journal*, the *National Review*, *Time*, and *Saturday Night*. On television, he is a regular panellist on CBC's *The National*, and was a co-host of the CBC public-affairs show *Face-Off*. He is the winner of two National Newspaper Awards and the Hyman Solomon Award for Excellence in Public Policy Journalism.

Tom Flanagan is a professor of political science at the University of Calgary. His book *First Nations? Second Thoughts* (2000) received an award from the Canadian Political Science Association for the best book of the year on Canadian politics. He has been an expert witness for the Crown in important native-rights cases such as Blais, Benoit, Chief Victor Buffalo, and Manitoba Metis Federation.

David Frum is the author most recently of *Comeback: Conservatism That Can Win Again*. He is a fellow of the American Enterprise Institute, a contributing editor to *National Review*, and a senior foreign-policy adviser to the Rudy Giuliani presidential campaign. In 2001–02, he served as a special assistant and speechwriter to President George W. Bush.

Robert Fulford has been a journalist since 1950. For nineteen years he was editor of *Saturday Night* magazine. At various times he has written a column in the *Toronto Star*, the *Globe and Mail*, the *Financial Times of Canada*, and *Maclean's*. Since 1999 he has been contributing to the *National Post*, where he writes every Tuesday and Saturday. He also writes in every issue of the *Queen's Quarterly*. He is an officer of the Order of Canada and a senior fellow of Massey College in the University of Toronto.

Allan Gotlieb had a distinguished career in the foreign services, including acting as Canada's ambassador to Washington from 1981 to 1989. He is currently senior advisor to the law firm Bennett Jones LLP.

Historian **J.L. Granatstein** writes on Canadian defence and foreign policy. His most recent book is *Whose War Is It?* (HarperCollins, 2007), and he is a fellow of the Canadian Defence and Foreign Affairs Institute.

Dr. David Gratzer, a physician, is licensed in both Canada and the United States. He is a senior fellow at the Manhattan Institute. His writing has graced the pages of more than a dozen newspapers and magazines, including the *Wall Street Journal*, the *Globe and Mail*, the *Los Angeles Times*, and *Maclean's*. He is the author of *Code Blue*, awarded the Donner Prize for best Canadian public-policy book in 2000. His most recent book is *The Cure*, with a foreword by Nobel laureate Milton Friedman.

Joel Kotkin is a Presidential Fellow in Urban Futures at Chapman University in southern California. He is author of *The City: A Global History* (Modern Library, 2006) and is working on a book on America's future. He has consulted widely in the United States for cities including New York, Los Angeles, Phoenix, Houston, and St. Louis. He has lectured widely in the United States, Canada, East Asia, Europe, and Australia, and has co-authored a paper on Laval's future with Rémy Tremblay of the Université de Québec.

Jessica LeCroy recently retired from the U.S. Diplomatic Corps to join the private sector. She was a Visiting Senior Fellow in Geoeconomics at the Council of Foreign Relations in New York from 2006 to 2008 and U.S. Consul General in Toronto from 2004 to 2006. She served on details from the Department of State as National Security Advisor to the Secretary of the Treasury and as senior legislative assistant for foreign policy and trade to Senator Bill Bradley. Overseas assignments included Iraq, Georgia, Bosnia, the Netherlands, and Nicaragua. She practised corporate and banking law before government service. The views expressed in her essay are entirely her own, and do not reflect U.S. government policy.

Patrick Luciani is currently co-director of the Salon Speakers Series in Toronto and senior resident at Massey College at the University of Toronto. He has written extensively on public policy issues and is currently co-authoring a book on health, technology and economics.

Neil Reynolds is national affairs editor for the *Globe and Mail*'s *Report on Business* and writes two columns a week on economic policy. His career as a journalist spans forty years. A senior editor at the *Toronto Star* for eight years, he served as editor-in-chief of major daily newspapers from coast-to-coast, including the *Ottawa Citizen*, the *Vancouver Sun*, the *Kingston Whig-Standard*, and the *Telegraph-Journal*, the Saint John-based provincial newspaper of New Brunswick. Newspapers edited by him won many honours for quality journalism, among them a number of National Newspaper Awards, the Michener Award for Public Service Journalism (three times), and the Canadian Journalism Foundation's Excellence in Journalism Award (two times). He now lives on a farm in the Lanark Highlands near Ottawa with his wife, *Ottawa Citizen* columnist Donna Jacobs.

ABOUT THE EDITOR

Rudyard Griffiths is the co-director of the Salon Speakers Series. Rudyard is also the co-founder of the Canadian think tank the Dominion Institute and is an advisor to the Woodrow Wilson Center in Washington, D.C. He writes a regular column on Canadian issues and international affairs for Canada's highest circulation paper, *The Toronto Star*. He has edited various books on Canadian history and politics. Griffiths serves on the boards of the Stratford Festival and Adrienne Clarkson's Canadian Institute for Citizenship. In 2006, he was recognized as one of Canada's Top 40 under 40. He is a graduate of Emmanual College, Cambridge.